Functional Analytic Psychotherapy

D0023849

How can I *supercharge* the therapy I currently use?

This volume distils the core principles, methods, and vision of the approach. Each Functinal Analytic Psychotherapy (FAP) principle is presented in terms of its intended purpose and is clearly linked to the underlying theory, thus providing clinicians with a straightforward guide for when and how to apply each technique.

FAP embraces awareness, courage, and love as integral to the treatment process. Part 1 of this volume reviews the history of FAP and the basic behavioral principles on which it is based. Part 2 provides an easy to use step-by-step guide to the application of FAP techniques.

FAP is an approach undergoing a renaissance, and this volume uniquely summarizes the full history, theory, and techniques of FAP, resulting in a handbook perfect for clinicians and graduate students with or without a behavioral background.

Mavis Tsai is a psychologist in independent practice and Director of the FAP Specialty Clinic at the University of Washington where she is involved in teaching and research.

Robert J. Kohlenberg is a Professor of Psychology at the University of Washington where he was a Director of Clinical Training.

Jonathan W. Kanter is Associate Professor and Clinic Coordinator at the Department of Psychology, and a Research Scholar at the

Center for Addictions and Behavioral Health, University of Wisconsin-Milwaukee.

Gareth I. Holman, Ph.D., was Bob Kohlenberg's last graduate student at the University of Washington, where he was trained in Functional Analytic Psychotherapy and Dialectical Behavior Therapy. He is now a postdoctoral fellow at the Evidence-Based Practice Institute in Seattle, WA, where he develops and conducts research on therapist trainings and other tools to support evidence-based practice. He continues to be involved in FAP training at the University of Washington and beyond.

Mary Plummer Loudon is a clinical psychologist in private practice and FAP Clinic supervisor at the University of Washington.

Cognitive-behaviour therapy (CBT) occupies a central position in the move towards evidence-based practice and is frequently used in the clinical environment. Yet there is no one universal approach to CBT and clinicians speak of first-, second-, and even third-wave approaches.

This series provides straightforward, accessible guides to a number of CBT methods, clarifying the distinctive features of each approach. The series editor, Windy Dryden, successfully brings together experts from each discipline to summarise the 30 main aspects of their approach divided into theoretical and practical features.

The CBT Distinctive Features Series will be essential reading for psychotherapists, counsellors, and psychologists of all orientations who want to learn more about the range of new and developing cognitive-behavioural approaches.

Titles in the series:

Acceptance and Commitment Therapy by Paul E. Flaxman, J.T. Blackledge and Frank W. Bond

Beck's Cognitive Therapy by Frank Wills

Behavioral Activation by Jonathan Kanter, Andrew M. Busch and Laura C. Rusch

Compassion Focused Therapy by Paul Gilbert

Constructivist Psychotherapy by Robert A. Neimeyer

Dialectical Behaviour Therapy by Michaela A. Swales and Heidi L. Heard

Functional Analytic Psychotherapy by Mavis Tsai, Robert J. Kohlenberg, Jonathan W. Kanter, Gareth I. Holman, and Mary Plummer Loudon

Metacognitive Therapy by Peter Fisher and Adrian Wells

Mindfulness-Based Cognitive Therapy by Rebecca Crane

Rational Emotive Behaviour Therapy by Windy Dryden

Schema Therapy by Eshkol Rafaeli, David P. Bernstein, and Jeffrey Young

For further information about this series, please visit www.routledgementalhealth.com/cbt-distinctive-features

Functional Analytic Psychotherapy

Distinctive Features

**Mavis Tsai,
Robert J. Kohlenberg,
Jonathan W. Kanter,
Gareth I. Holman, and
Mary Plummer Loudon**

Routledge
Taylor & Francis Group

HOVE AND NEW YORK

First published 2012 by Routledge
27 Church Road, Hove, East Sussex BN3 2FA

Simultaneously published in the USA and Canada
by Routledge
711 Third Avenue, New York NY 10017

Routledge is an imprint of the Taylor & Francis Group, an Informa business

British Library Cataloguing in Publication Data
A catalogue record for this book is available from the British Library

Library of Congress Cataloging in Publication Data
Functional analytic psychotherapy : distinctive features / Mavis Tsai . . . [et al.].
     p. cm. — (The CBT distinctive features series)
   Includes bibliographical references and index.
   ISBN 978-0-415-60403-1 (hardback: alk. paper) — ISBN 978-0-415-60404-8
   (pbk.: alk. paper)   1. Behavior therapy.   2. Psychoanalysis.   I. Tsai, Mavis.
   RC489.B4F86 2012
   616.89'142—dc23
                                                            2011042903

ISBN: 978-0-415-60404-8 (pbk)
ISBN: 978-0-415-60403-1 (hbk)
ISBN: 978-0-203-12115-3 (ebk)

Cover design by Sandra Heath
Typeset in Times
by RefineCatch Limited, Bungay, Suffolk

Contents

Preface

Functional Analytic Psychotherapy (FAP) is a behavioral approach based on empirically supported principles that harnesses the power of the therapeutic relationship and maximizes the genuineness, intensity, compassion, and effectiveness of the therapist. FAP therapists view each client as a micro-culture with complex life stories of joy and anguish, dreams and hopes, passions and vulnerabilities, and unique gifts and abilities, carrying deeply rooted cultural, social, and generational experiences in their reinforcement histories. From a behaviorally defined perspective, the qualities of awareness, courage, and therapeutic love are considered by FAP therapists to be the building blocks of a therapeutic bond that is the springboard for client change.

The importance of the therapeutic relationship is not unique to FAP. This emphasis is asserted in all CBT (Cognitive Behavioral Therapy) approaches, although none elevates it to the central role it has in FAP. The difficulty is that nearly everyone means something different by the concept of the therapeutic relationship, and it has a history of nuances and definitions that dates back to Sigmund Freud. Given these complexities and often deeply held preconceptions, our challenge is to present the FAP viewpoint briefly and yet clearly distinguish it from existing notions. Thus, this book distils the core principles, techniques, and vision of FAP into 30 short points that emphasize its power as a precise behavioral theory leading to flexible, compassionate, intimate, and powerful therapeutic relationships that supercharge any CBT treatment. The points are written to maximize clarity and understanding for all readers, including those without a behavioral background, those who wish to add FAP techniques to their ongoing work, and those already familiar with FAP wishing to expand their expertise.

Part 1 of this volume reviews the history of FAP and the basic behavioral principles on which it is based. As we explain how contingent reinforcement, a well-established empirically supported mechanism of change, accounts for the centrality of the client–therapist relationship to the change process, we address common misconceptions about reinforcement (e.g., it involves therapist reactions such as saying "that's good" or other such artificial reactions). Instead we show how reinforcement occurs naturally (often out of awareness) during the give-and-take of the therapist–client interaction. We address in concrete terms how therapists can position themselves to be naturally reinforcing of client improvements. Perhaps somewhat unexpectedly, we also discuss one facet of natural reinforcement we call "therapeutic love," exploring from a behavioral perspective how this notion applies to and can be useful in almost any type of therapy. Part 2 provides a step-by-step guide to the application of FAP techniques and rules. Each FAP rule and technique is presented in terms of its intended function, so each technique is clearly linked to the underlying theory, providing clinicians with not just a description of the technique but a simple guide for when and how to use each one.

An advantage to the behavioral approach is that its concepts are well defined and thus hold the promise of being clearly understandable. Nevertheless, misunderstandings abound about behaviorism, and in turn, many therapists incorrectly see it as narrow and mechanical. Likewise, behavioral techniques sometimes have been seen as too simple to treat complex conditions. This book presents behavioral theory and FAP techniques in terms that clarify their purpose and show how they can lead to deep, intense therapeutic relationships with pragmatic examples demonstrating the utility of this approach for both simple and complex cases.

Given the potential importance of the therapeutic relationship to help therapists of any theoretical persuasion achieve the goals of their approach, this book contains concrete suggestions about how to intensify here-and-now therapeutic interactions. Consistent with an integrationist emphasis, specific guidelines are given so that therapists can use FAP concepts along with existing CBT treatments to deal with a wide range of significant clinical issues such as intimacy, problems of the self, and attachment.

FAP is undergoing a renaissance and is imbued with a new sense of purpose. Recent research has suggested that FAP's mechanism of change is valid and can lead to marked changes in clients. FAP training and workshops regularly produce marked and lasting transformative changes in therapist behavior, leading to great interest and excitement in new material on FAP. With more research and training planned over the next several years, we expect to see an explosion of interest in FAP as these results come to light. Whatever your orientation, wherever you are in your individual journey as a psychotherapist, we hope that the ideas and information contained in this book will inspire you intellectually and facilitate therapeutic relationships that are extraordinary and unforgettable.

Acknowledgements

Mavis Tsai:

I have the utmost of love and respect for my dream team of co-authors. They are each treasures I truly cherish. Bob is the universe's greatest blessing to me. His love is the most magnificent I have ever experienced, and has taught me how to love beyond what I imagined my capabilities to be. Without his profound intellect, FAP would not exist. I count on him to challenge me daily to be a better clinician, teacher, and person. His belief in me sustains me in all my endeavors. He is the love of my life. Jonathan's eloquence suffuses his intellect, his heart, and his life's work. He has a sophisticated and unique understanding of Bob's and my perspective on FAP that no one else has. His research on FAP is brilliant and groundbreaking. Gareth is a talented and wise FAP theorist and therapist far beyond his years; his thinking and work are deep and refined. I am thrilled to have him as a colleague as he enters the postdoctoral world. Mary has become part of my innermost circle through 6 years of co-teaching the University of Washington FAP practicum with me. I rely on her clinical acumen and power as a FAP leader, and I deeply appreciate how she consistently models authenticity, insight, and expressiveness. Her presence in my life is like a perpetual sunrise.

I would like to acknowledge Windy Dryden, CBT Distinctive Features Editor, for suggesting that FAP be included in this series. We are honored to be recognized in this way. I would also like to thank Nancy Brainard for her expert editing of the final draft of our manuscript.

More than anyone else, Sijo John Beall, founder of Tsun Jo Wing Chun Kung Fu, has taught me to look fear directly in the eye. Due to his exceptional tutelage the past 15 years, I embody boldness and courage.

Finally, I am indebted to all my students, trainees, and clients past and present. They have shaped and reinforced the best of who I am, and are responsible for my commitment to FAP. They each occupy a space in my heart that is uniquely their own.

Robert J. Kohlenberg:

I first wish to acknowledge my beloved Mavis whose love not only has nourished and sustained me for more than three decades, but is also intimately intertwined in the development of FAP and our life journey. Her magical therapeutic work was the initial inspiration for FAP, and in combination with her astonishing intellect, our love, and many very heated discussions, FAP was born. The process has continued since that time and I am still inspired by her clinical and intellectual genius and love that has brought FAP far beyond its origins. I adore her.

Jonathan Kanter, who early on as my student, was the first to see the potential contribution that FAP could make to our field. Since I knew he was brilliant, his vision in turn affirmed my commitment to FAP. He pushed for and played a key role in developing the research that was central to gaining the attention of the scientific community. He and his colleagues have continued in this vein and accomplished the laborious and difficult task of empirically testing and confirming the underlying mechanism of change that is at the core of FAP. He is a prolific scientist, author, and professor who has inspired many others to contribute to our field. His lab at the University of Wisconsin in Milwaukee is a center for FAP training and research. I deeply value his continued collaboration with me, his values, and am honored to have him as friend.

Mary Plummer Loudon, who truly is a master FAP therapist, has that same "magic" that inspired the creation of FAP. She not only contributes to the published literature on FAP but has taken on a major training role in helping to produce the next generation of FAP researchers and therapists. She is an inspiring teacher who projects her competence and warmth to all who come in contact with her. I feel it every time I see her and am thankful she is my colleague.

Gareth Holman has the distinction of being my last student. His brilliance, breadth of knowledge, creativity, and deep analytical thinking are obvious and compelling. His research is groundbreaking and he plays an important role in training FAP therapists. He is a talented writer who already has contributed to the FAP literature, and in the future he will use this talent to disseminate FAP not only to professionals but also to the world at large. His gentle challenging of my ideas has added to my growth and I am looking forward to our continued collaboration and friendship.

I also wish to acknowledge those who have played an important role in my development as a clinical behavior analyst—Loren Acker, Steven C. Hayes, Barbara Kohlenberg, Marsha Linehan, and the late Ivar Lovaas, Neil Jacobson, and Alan Marlatt.

Jonathan W. Kanter:
I would like to acknowledge Bob Kohlenberg and Mavis Tsai, for whom my respect and love grow with each new project we collectively approach and accomplish. My wife Gwynne Kohl continues to be the foundation without which I could not thrive as a professional, and my daughter Zoe has become the inspiration for almost all I do. I would also like to acknowledge the amazing group of graduate students I have had the pleasure to mentor. Finally, it is cliched but absolutely necessary to acknowledge how much I have learned from the clinicians and clients who have trusted me with their training and healing. I hope our work honors their trust.

Gareth I. Holman:
I appreciate my co-authors for being so exciting and inspiring—yet simultaneously efficient and balanced.

I would like to recognize the whole FAP community, especially the graduate students involved in the FAP practicum at the University of Washington. We have something very special, and I look forward to years of collaboration.

Finally, and above all, I would like to acknowledge Bob Kohlenberg and Mavis Tsai. I did not realize when I received admission to the University of Washington doctoral program, under the primary mentorship of Bob, that I was in fact receiving a mentorship "two-for-one" deal. I feel blessed to have received their wisdom, their belief in me, and their patience and care in challenging my shortcomings these last 6 years. It seems obvious—though it is true—to say that I would not have completed graduate school without them. It feels truer in my bones to say that I would not be who I am without them.

Mary Plummer Loudon:

It is an understatement to say that Mavis and Bob have shaped who I am as a clinician today. The truth is that they have shaped much more than merely my professional identity or my theoretical orientation—they have been closer to second parents to me in their mentorship, encouragement, guidance, support, and faithful stimulation of my emotions and intellect. Their awareness, courage, and love have grown my heart and, on behalf of myself and every person whose life I touch, I thank you both.

I am grateful for the many unforgettable students I have met over the years through the FAP Practicum and FAP Clinic at the University of Washington. I have learned as much from them as I hope to have taught them, and they deserve the credit for shaping me into a better supervisor, group facilitator, therapist, and FAP trainer. Every week they provided me the opportunity to play FAP jazz with them, deepening my appreciation for its underlying principles and helping me create new language, metaphors, and exercises to teach FAP. I hope they will continue to contribute to the development and dissemination of FAP and realize themselves as leaders in the FAP community.

Part 1

THE DISTINCTIVE THEORETICAL FEATURES OF FAP

1

The historical roots of Functional Analytic Psychotherapy

Three strands account for the origin of Functional Analytic Psychotherapy (FAP). First, most practicing therapists report a surprising and remarkable finding. Even when following a manual and using standardized procedures, some of our clients achieve gains that go far beyond the intended goal of symptom alleviation or of obtaining remission from a *DSM*-defined disorder (*Diagnostic and Statistical Manual of Mental Disorders IV*, American Psychiatric Association, 2000). We will refer to these phenomena as "exceptionally good outcomes." Most of us, especially in this era of empirically supported treatments, do help most of our clients. The phenomena we are talking about, however, go beyond this usual "good" outcome. (Although most patients are helped, needless to say, the obverse side of these exceptionally good outcomes are those clients for whom the same methods that seem to help others are mysteriously unsuccessful.)

Second, the exceptionally good outcomes seem to occur only occasionally, and it is difficult for the therapist to specify what is responsible for their occurrence in a way that is coherent and sensible to others. If we could do this specification, then we would be able to achieve exceptionally good outcomes more frequently. There are, of course, large individual differences such that some therapists seem to obtain these exceptionally good outcomes more frequently than others. For example, author RJK considered himself a competent CBT (Cognitive Behavioral Therapy) therapist who achieved good treatment results. In the course of the first 10 years of his career before FAP, however, he had about six exceptionally good outcomes. Conversely, most of author MT's clients frequently reached these heights, seemingly independent of the model of treatment that she used. Just as there are individual differences in therapists, individual differences in clients affect outcome. The exceptionally good outcomes we are referring to are beyond those we might attribute to client characteristics.

Third, in our experience and in interviewing colleagues about what was different about these exceptional cases, one commonality emerged that captured these exceptional cases. Intensity, personal involvement, and frequent moment-to-moment therapist–client exchanges made these clients and the therapy experiences unforgettable. There was something special in the therapist–client relationship. The therapist–client relationship frequently is invoked to explain differential outcomes (e.g., Horvath, 2001), however, exactly how and why the therapeutic relationship affects outcome and what the therapist can do to influence this relationship in order to obtain these exceptional outcomes are less well-specified. For this reason, and for want of a better word, we will temporarily refer to this difficult-to-describe quality as "magic" in the therapy room.

If you are concerned that our use of the term "magic" means we believe there are mysterious, new age, perhaps paranormal phenomena that therapists must learn to harness, nothing could be farther from the truth. Further, we do not believe that master therapists have the magic spark and the rest of us are doomed to do "good" but not "exceptional" work. Instead, our task is to understand what kinds of therapist actions (interventions) bring about the phenomena that seem magical. Our recommendations must be well-specified, easy to understand, and easily teachable to others.

We turned to behaviorism as a means of accomplishing these goals. Behaviorism has the advantages of a strong laboratory empirical base, operationally defined concepts, and precise language. These advantages establish a theory that in turn produces effective techniques that can be taught precisely to others. The result of this endeavor is FAP.

FAP is not the first to use behavioral concepts to define an exceptionally effective but somewhat mysterious and unteachable clinical treatment. C. B. Ferster (1967), an early behaviorist, studied an extremely talented therapist who obtained amazing results in her treatment of autistic children. Others who tried to emulate her were not effective. Her approach was purely intuitive, and she could not coherently describe why she did what she did. Dr Ferster intensively observed her work over a long period of time. He used behavioral concepts to describe what she did as well as to account for her amazing effects. Needless to say, this process led to an understandable, nonmysterious, and, most important, teachable treatment that was the forerunner of today's treatment practices for severely disturbed children.

Another advantage of using behaviorism to explain why and how exceptional outcomes are obtained is that it does not suffer from the downfall of other similar attempts to capture the essential elements of why some therapists do better than others. Most notably, there is a long-standing tradition in our field of studying "master therapists," those who routinely help clients achieve exceptionally good outcomes (Shapiro, 1987). The process entails studying the superstar therapist, observing what s/he does, and then teaching others to emulate it. The downfall, according to Shapiro, is that imitating the exact behaviors of a successful therapist does not take into account that what works for one therapist may not work for another. In contrast, the process used by Ferster, described above, developed general abstract principles that accommodated contextual differences between therapists and clients (i.e., used functional analysis as discussed later in this book) and avoided the "one size fits all" problem.

Similarly, FAP is not a set of specific procedures. Instead, it is a set of general principles based on behaviorism. It is important to emphasize, however, that in order to implement FAP, you do not have to be a behaviorist. Although FAP can be used as a stand-alone therapy, our quantitative and qualitative data indicate that FAP easily can be integrated and bring intensity and "magic" to any other therapeutic approach.

2

Appreciations and misunderstandings of behaviorism

Much ink has been spilled arguing about the validity and usefulness of behaviorism—ranging from statements that "behaviorism is dead" (e.g., Behavior Analysis Association of Michigan, n.d.) to claims that Skinner is the most influential psychologist of the 20th century (Haggbloom et al., 2002). In fact, despite regular proclamations of its death, behaviorism continues to flourish in psychology and beyond. For example, attendance at ABAI (Association for Behavior Analysis International) meetings continues to grow each year, books on behavioral economics reach the top of best-seller lists, and treatments based on behavioral concepts are among the most widely disseminated evidence-based treatments.

How is it possible for behaviorism to be so vehemently rejected by so many of our colleagues, while at the same time establishing an enthusiastic following by others as well as a clearly demonstrable record of achievement? A key to understanding this conundrum has to do with widespread core misunderstandings of behaviorism.

The core misunderstanding: behaviorists view people as black-box automatons

When asked what the word "behaviorism" brings to mind, a colleague responded, "I have a visceral sense of rejection. I think it's simplistic, and it denies the reality of a rich complex inner psyche that interacts with external reality. Behaviorism has always seemed very arrogant to me, in the sense that the incredible mystery of being has been reduced to what can be observed."

The idea that behaviorism is simplistic and reduces meaningful behavior to only that which can be observed is a core misunderstanding that many of our colleagues hold. This distortion occurs because many clinicians are not aware that there are two markedly different meanings of the term behaviorism, much less what the distinction is between these. The first meaning, referred to as "methodological behaviorism," is based on Watson's (1930) contention that the science of behavior is possible if the subject matter being studied is defined by its observable forms, such as muscle movements and glandular secretions. Methodological behaviorism requires public agreement for observations. It thus excludes introspection and the direct study of consciousness, feelings, and thinking, by focusing on only what is publicly observable. Unfortunately, this outdated methodological behaviorism is the type of behaviorism of which most of our colleagues are aware.

The second meaning of behaviorism stems from B. F. Skinner and is known as "radical behaviorism." In 1945, Skinner (Boring, Bridgman, Feigl, Pratt, & Skinner, 1945) differentiated his approach from the rest of psychology by declaring that his "toothache is just as physical as my typewriter" (p. 294) and rejected both the requirement of public agreement and the tenets of methodological behaviorism. Radical behaviorism rejected stimulus–response psychology, and instead, based on an understanding of verbal behavior, included the private world (e.g., thoughts, feelings, sensations) in the realm of a science of behavior.

A comment is in order about behaviorism and viewing a person as an "automaton," a type of machine. Man as a machine represents a philosophical worldview referred to as "mechanism," and is the philosophical underpinning of methodological behaviorism. In contrast, radical behaviorism explicitly rejects the mechanistic worldview and is based on the philosophical approach known as "contextualism." It calls for explanations of why we act the way we do to take into account the unique history of the individual up to that moment in time (Hayes, Hayes, & Reese, 1988).

This history of the individual not only includes our experiences in the last 24 hours but extends all the way back into infancy. The requirement that behavior has meaning only if it includes its historical context has led Hayes (Hayes & Hayes, 1992) to suggest that we use the term "contextualistic behaviorism" instead of "radical behaviorism" to describe Skinner's approach. Today, we have behavioral analyses of the entire range of human experience—including, for example, language, feeling, self, perceiving, acting, remembering, cognition, emotion, intimacy, and empathy.

An appreciation of behaviorism (contextual behaviorism)

Radical or contextual behaviorism is a psychology solidly rooted in concrete events occurring in the world. The contextual behavioral psychologist attempts to divine the relations among these events in order to predict and influence the future. That is, behaviorism is committed to studying the subtleties and realities of our complex histories, to understanding the ways that events, including feelings and thoughts, interact over the course of people's lives to produce particular ways of being (i.e., behaving) today. It should be clear from this account that behaviorism does *not* assume that we are empty automatons responding mechanically and uniformly to external stimuli. Rather, behaviorism is a powerful way of *understanding individuality*. Perhaps because of this emphasis on individuality, behaviorism is also a way of truly *empathizing with and being non-judgmental of others*. Is there a better way of understanding another human being than by hearing his or her entire story or history? It is no accident that radical behavioral therapies are so concordant with acceptance-based approaches to therapy.

When behaviorism is viewed as a contextualistic approach (radical behaviorism), it offers scientifically valid concepts that are useful and effective for accomplishing goals that people care about. Clarification of misunderstandings leads to a basic appreciation of what behaviorism offers us (to be expanded upon in later points) as clinicians and researchers. This entire book, in fact, may be read as an extended appreciation of behaviorism—how behaviorism makes us not only more effective scientists, but also more effective human beings, more able to understand and care for those around us.

3

The importance of environments and history

What causes behavior? There are of course many ways to answer this question, and almost all psychologists would agree that any complex, clinically interesting human behavior is caused by multiple factors. The major domains of causes typically are: genetic, biological, cognitive, environmental, and personality. FAP's behavioral worldview focuses on environmental causes of behavior, which include both the client's current environment and the client's history of interactions with the environment.

To a behaviorist, the meaning of a behavior is to be found in the current environmental contingencies that support the behavior and the historical contingencies that shaped the behavior. We are a product both of our current and of our past environments. Any clinically relevant behavior is to be understood in these terms. The current environment includes the immediate setting (the therapy room, the therapy relationship), the client's current relationships, and larger ethnic-cultural and political forces that influence our behavior. The past simply includes everything that has come before. While certain features of a client's history may be emphasized (traumatic events, family relationships), isolating certain historical events from the stream of history that has shaped us is somewhat of an arbitrary process—definitely useful for therapeutic purposes but not to be confused with a full analysis of the myriad past and present influences on our behavior.

This focus results in particular stances with respect to how other causes should be viewed. First, genetics certainly play a role in determining and constraining behavior. A FAP therapist, therefore, has an appreciation for the genetic vulnerabilities and risks that a client has inherited, but does not focus on genetics as causes. This is largely a pragmatic issue—focusing on genetic causes does not give the therapist much to do, as genetic causes cannot be manipulated therapeutically (at least not with the kinds of interventions we are interested in). Furthermore, considerable research demonstrates that focusing on genetic causes makes individuals less hopeful about the possibility that they can change their behavior, more likely to look to pharmacological solutions to behavior problems, and more likely to view hospitalization as the primary treatment setting (e.g., Mehta & Farina, 1997; Read & Harre, 2001). Thus, focusing on genetics is generally ineffective for adult, outpatient psychotherapy, as research indicates that such an emphasis makes it harder to do the work of therapy.

From a broad philosophical rather than pragmatic standpoint, a FAP therapist actually sees genetic causes as environmental causes. Our genes, after all, are a product of interactions with the environment. Just as a FAP therapist believes that reinforcement shapes and strengthens the behaviors in our current repertoire, natural selection has shaped our genetic blueprint into what it is today. Our genes are a summary of the shaping processes that have occurred before our birth. Ultimately, therefore, the environment is the causal agent even for genetics. The current behavior of an individual is a function of the environmental contingencies of reinforcement that have shaped the behavior of the individual and the environmental contingencies of survival that have shaped the behavior of the species.

Biology is another matter. To a behaviorist, biological and environmental explanations for behavior are not competing explanations; they are parallel, compatible explanations offered at different levels of analysis. All behavior, after all, requires ongoing biological support. Any change in behavior will be represented as neurobiological change, and predictable brain changes should be identifiable over the course of therapy, as researchers are beginning to demonstrate (Dichter et al., 2009).

Biological explanations for behavior are extremely popular today, and for good reason. The brain fascinates and amazes, and technological advances in brain science are providing increasingly detailed understandings of brain functioning. To a FAP therapist, however, focusing on biological explanations of behavior, like focusing on genetics, is not pragmatic. Biological constructs are not particularly helpful to a FAP case conceptualization and, in fact, can confuse matters. A good FAP therapist, like any professional psychologist, should be knowledgeable about when neuropsychological assessment may be a helpful resource in understanding and treating a client, but in general a FAP case conceptualization will not focus on biological or neuropsychological variables because to do so steers attention away from environmental reinforcement as a mechanism of behavior change.

Cognition, discussed more fully in Point 12, is another matter as well. To a FAP therapist, cognition is behavior. Thinking, daydreaming, planning, wondering, reasoning, interpreting, believing, and so forth, are things people do, and a behaviorist would look to the same current and historical environmental explanations for these sorts of behaviors as for other sorts of behaviors. Offering a cognitive explanation of behavior, to a behaviorist, is equivalent to saying, "this behavior caused that behavior" (Hayes & Brownstein, 1986). It is not much of an explanation until causes *outside* the behavioral system are identified. Furthermore, the full cognitive theory introduces cognitive constructs, namely schemas, that are not translatable as behavior at all. These constructs, to behaviorists, are hypothetical, mentalistic inventions. Unlike biology and behavior, in which one level of analysis is reducible to another level, cognition and behavior are not compatible, parallel analyses. Cognitive theory and behavioral theory are incompatible, and a behaviorist instead would look to behavioral theory to understand cognition.

Personality as a cause is similar to cognition as a cause to a FAP therapist. Personality reflects some admixture of: (1) behavioral repertoires that recur predictably and thus are labeled as personality ("She is very social and therefore has an 'outgoing' personality"); (2) mentalistic inventions that are at best redundant with behavior ("He is addicted to drugs because of his addictive personality") or at worst are lacking behavioral referents altogether [(e.g., a certain profile score on an MMPI (Minnesota Multiphasic Personality Iventory)] examination). Thus, personality constructs rarely play a role in FAP case conceptualizations.

Having reframed, discarded as not pragmatic, or discarded as mentalistic fictions most constructs from genetics, biology, cognitive science, and personality theory, is it a wonder that behaviorists sometimes have a hard time gaining respect from their colleagues who have devoted their careers to studying these issues?

The authors have felt these strains. The challenge to the reader is: Is it worth it? The priority, from Skinner's earliest writings, was to develop a psychological worldview that maximized the chance that our scientific thinking and analyses would have a positive impact on our world. Skinner (1976) said:

The choice is clear: either we do nothing and allow a miserable and probably catastrophic future to overtake us, or we use our knowledge about human behavior to create a social environment in which we shall live productive and creative lives and do so without jeopardizing the chances that those who follow us will be able to do the same. (p. xvi, emphasis added)

As FAP therapists, we believe that the behavioral worldview, which indeed has not made us many friends and has alienated many, is the best available perspective upon which a therapy system can be built. Unlike genetic, biological, cognitive, or personality science, which were developed to discover truth, behavioral science is the only scientific system that was engineered from the beginning to be helpful to the consumers of the science (Skinner, 1953). The behavioral worldview clarifies and focuses the therapist on variables that can impact the client in the here and now and does not get distracted by variables that are not potentially impactful. It should lead to a more powerful therapeutic relationship that creates positive behavior change in our clients' lives.

4

What's the function?

Your client has not completed any of the homework assignments you and she collaboratively developed in the last session. How do you as a therapist respond?

Many cognitive-behavioral therapies assign homework, and FAP is no exception. Typically, homework completion is to be praised. The therapist may react with genuine pleasure to such behavior, and with good reason. In group research designs, homework completion has been shown to predict positive therapeutic outcomes (Kazantzis & Lampropoulos, 2002). Thus, if a client does not complete any homework, a logical response might be to express compassionate disappointment and review with the client the importance of homework completion to therapy.

In FAP, however, we want to look deeper, to the function of the behavior, rather than respond solely on the basis of form. Determining behavioral function involves exploring two broad sets of questions about the behavior of interest:

1   What are the contexts that evoke the behavior?
2   What are the consequences that make it more or less likely?

In this client's case, we may wonder or ask about contexts in which homework is completed. When and where is it most likely to happen? Is this a rare occurrence of not doing homework, or does the client have a strong history of not doing homework (e.g., in school)? Is homework completion a function of the person who assigns the homework (a doctor, a therapist, a teacher)? Is s/he more likely to complete homework if s/he is not distracted by the family at home?

Thinking next about consequences, we may wonder or ask about consequences that have followed homework completion in the past.

Have teachers or other authority figures actually punished previous attempts at homework completion as "not good enough," or has effort over perfection been reinforced? Does the client have a long history of receiving praise for doing what authority figures (e.g., therapists) want (e.g., homework completion)? Has the client learned from previous relationships that care will be withdrawn when s/he is functioning well, such that homework completion may be punished by the therapist by concluding that s/he does not need therapy anymore?

Such an analysis leads to several possibilities, each of which may be responded to differently by a FAP therapist. Perhaps the client, with a long history of pleasing others, has chosen this moment to take a risk by behaving in a way that will not produce praise. If so, homework incompletion may actually be an improvement (see Point 8 on clinically relevant behaviors). Alternately, perhaps the client may be scared to turn in homework to the therapist, for fear it will not be good enough. If so, homework incompletion may be a problem as it is typically viewed. Perhaps the client is usually quite responsible, but this week a child was sick and s/he was simply preoccupied? If so, homework incompletion is not clinically relevant.

Most therapists will want to explore why a client did not complete homework before blindly responding to homework incompletion as a problem. The FAP analysis simply adds structure to this exploration, focusing on behavioral function as the key to understanding why, and—as we will discuss in Part 2 of this book—linking specific therapist responses to the behavioral functions identified.

All clinically relevant behavior in FAP is to be understood functionally in this way. What is the function of a client's crying, anger, request, or focus on certain topics in session? Out of session, what is the function of the client's behavior of staying at home all day, looking for a new job, or acting seductively at a party? The question, "What's the function?" may be the most important question to a FAP therapist, as it is fundamental to FAP's Rule 1 [(Watch for CRBs (clinically relevant behaviors), see Points 18 and 19].

5

Understanding the functions of the therapist

In FAP, asking "What's the function?" applies both to client behavior and therapist behavior. The FAP therapist is most interested in the functions of his or her own behavior that impact the client. As discussed in Point 19, awareness of these functions is critical to Rule 1. Although a detailed understanding of functional analysis would suggest additional functions, FAP simplifies the analysis and focuses on three primary functional impacts the therapist may have on the client. That is, no matter what a therapist does, it can be viewed as presenting a stimulus during the session. Regardless of the theoretical orientation of the therapist, from our behavioral viewpoint, there are only three possible functions of these stimuli. Each of these is discussed below. Keep in mind that at any one moment, the stimulus presented by a therapist may have more than one function.

The therapist elicits client behavior

Elicited behavior is respondent or classically conditioned behavior. These responses feel automatic and involuntary, like reflexes. In experimental settings, we can have respondent behavior such as eye blinks in response to a puff of air, salivation in response to food in the mouth, and so forth. Classically conditioned behavior is similar: an eye blink in response to a noise that has been previously paired with a puff of air, salivation in response to the bell that has reliably preceded the food in the mouth.

In the therapy room, elicited behavior is often emotional. A client may start crying when she begins discussing an upcoming funeral. A man starts to experience panic when talking about a potential diagnosis of cancer. A client feels abandoned when the therapist does not remember his birthday. A woman becomes nervous at the beginning of the session because she does not know what to say.

Therapists are powerful elicitors, and this power is both verbal and non-verbal. Certainly, what we say matters, and sensitivity to nuanced elicited client reactions to our words is an important function in FAP. Furthermore, choosing words carefully, with sensitivity to their eliciting functions, is important in FAP. Much FAP language that is caring and compassionate, as expressed later in this book, is designed to elicit emotional responses in clients, and in therapists who may want to improve their abilities as FAP therapists.

Our non-verbal behavior also functions to elicit client responses. Our posture, how we pay attention, and especially eye contact are all relevant. In FAP, awareness of how we as therapists elicit client emotional behavior is of fundamental importance, and paying attention to this process is captured in FAP's Rule 1: Watch for clinically relevant behaviors (CRBs), which is discussed more fully in Points 18 and 19.

The therapist evokes client behavior

Evoked behavior is operant behavior, and FAP presumes that most clinically relevant behavior is operant. Almost everything a therapist does in session with a client calls for an operant response by the client. When a therapist asks a question to the client, an operant to respond, or perhaps to avoid, is prompted. When the therapist sits quietly and looks at the client, or says "um-hmm," an operant for the client to continue what s/he was doing is prompted. When the therapist hands a client a tissue, an operant for the client to take the tissue is prompted. When the therapist looks up at the clock and smiles gently, an operant for the client to recognize that time is almost up in the session is prompted.

Many client operant responses will be therapeutically useful, but from a FAP perspective we are particularly interested in operant responses that are clinically relevant. CRBs are client operant responses that occur in session, in response to the therapy setting, therapist, or therapy relationship, that are similar functionally to the client behaviors that occur out-of-session that are the focus of therapy for the client. CRBs are discussed more fully in Point 8.

Because of our particular interest in evoking CRBs, specific attention is paid to this process with FAP's Rule 2: Evoke CRBs. This is discussed more fully in Point 18 and Point 20.

The therapist consequates client behavior

Whether we are aware of it or not, we are continually providing consequences for (or *consequating*) one another's behavior. Consequences include both reinforcement and punishment. As discussed more fully in the next point, reinforcement is fundamental to human behavior and occurs continuously in human interaction. Using the examples of evoking behavior provided above, it is easy to show how a simple behavior may have multiple functions. When a therapist asks a client a question, in addition to prompting a response, the therapist may also be reinforcing client talk in general, by demonstrating interest. When listening to a client or responding with "um-hmm," a therapist may be reinforcing client talk as well, essentially letting the client know that s/he is understood and may continue. When handing a client a tissue, a therapist may be reinforcing client emotional expression in session. When looking up at the clock, the therapist may be gently punishing continued discussion.

In FAP, this reinforcement process is made explicit and harnessed for maximum client benefit. We not only notice when reinforcement is occurring, we strategically apply reinforcement to help the client (taking precautions to avoid arbitrary reinforcement, see Point 7). It is the key process in FAP. Much of this book is devoted to understanding how to establish a therapy relationship that focuses the therapist on natural reinforcement of client improvements, how to notice opportunities to provide reinforcement, how to reinforce specifically (and what not to do), and how to talk about the reinforcement process with clients after it has occurred.

The three therapist stimulus functions of eliciting, evoking, and consequating client behavior capture, from a functional standpoint, everything a therapist does in session. A reader, however, may be thinking that the primary thing s/he does in session is talk and may wonder where talking fits in to this scheme? Talking is clearly important to therapy, and to FAP, and is integrated into the treatment in several ways with CRB3s (see Point 8) and Rule 5 (see Points 18 and 24). We expect therapists to talk, to convey information that is useful to the client, to provide psycho-education, and so forth, as a primary behavior, formally defined. FAP, however, focuses the therapist on *what is happening functionally in the room, while therapeutic talk is occurring*. By paying attention to the three therapist stimulus functions as you are engaging in your typical therapeutic talk, you are ready to move into FAP process when opportunities for natural reinforcement present themselves.

6

The central role of reinforcement

Consider the following questions that a client might ask: "Why am I the way that I am?" "Why do I seem to get into such destructive relationships?" "Why am I so self-critical?" "Why do I have such low self-esteem?" or "Why am I preoccupied with thoughts and plans to kill myself?" There is, of course, an almost endless list of questions of this type.

Now let us say that you as a therapist are going to answer, but you are limited to a brief response, and further, your answer will be informed by a behavioral perspective. The answer then is, "because of the contingencies of reinforcement you have experienced." Needless to say, if you actually did give this answer, your client would most likely be utterly confused and perhaps consider getting another therapist. Further, without a more in-depth understanding of what is meant by "reinforcement" many therapists would consider the answer to be theoretically deficient. Nevertheless, this is the answer that underlies a core view of FAP, and once fully understood, will be very useful in guiding your therapeutic work.

In this point, we will spell out the essence of what is meant by reinforcement; in later points, we will discuss how this idea is put to practical use to intensify your therapeutic work and improve outcomes, regardless of the type therapy you do. By definition, contingencies are consequences—how the world (including both the physical and interpersonal world) responds to behavior—and at any given moment, the world is either strengthening (reinforcing) or not strengthening (punishing or extinguishing) a person's behavior by supplying consequences.

Contingencies of reinforcement are important because they are primary causes of our actions, which include everything that we do such as thinking, believing, noticing, perceiving, walking, eating, expressing feelings, and hiding feelings. Nevertheless, the importance of contingencies of reinforcement is frequently overlooked in the therapist–client interactions occurring throughout the therapy session.

Contingency means that when you act in a certain way, your action produces an effect or consequence. Often these effects occur in the physical world, for example, turning the ignition on in your car has the effect of starting the engine. Because this book is about helping clients, however, and almost all client problems involve interpersonal relating, the effects or consequences we focus on are the ways that others react to your interpersonal or social behavior. When you act in a certain way, and the effect that your action has on others makes it more or less likely that you will act in the same way in the future, the effect is referred to as a contingency of reinforcement. There are a few nuances, however, to the preceding statement. When the consequence makes it more likely that you will act in the same way again, it is called *positive reinforcement*. When the consequence makes it less likely that you will act in the same way again, it is called *punishment*. When there is no longer a consequence for an action that was positively reinforced in the past, you are less likely to keep acting that way. Your behavior will stop, and this effect is referred to as *extinction*.

Reinforcement is among one of the most studied and empirically evaluated concepts in psychology. Keep in mind, however, that "reinforcement" is just a word. Like any other word, it is understood from the context within which it is used. As used in FAP, reinforcement can be of great assistance to achieving the goals of psychotherapy regardless of the particular theoretical approach.

Reinforcement has two important qualities that when understood can help further its application as a broad principle: reinforcement is ubiquitous, and it typically occurs without awareness.

One way to understand our moment-to-moment daily experiences is through the lens of a behaviorist who views the stream of our actions and consequences from a reinforcement standpoint. Our current behavior is a function of the history of reinforcements that have shaped it in the past, just as the strength and width and shape of a stream at any one point are a function of the topography of the mountain from which it flowed. As we are behaving, reinforcement is constantly occurring, shaping our stream, making certain actions more likely and others less likely. Our future behavior, when it occurs, is a product of this history.

Typically, reinforcement has little to do with whether we are aware of having positive feelings after a particular action. A child learning to walk is not aware that each successful landing of a step reinforces the taking of it; a student learning to read may not be aware that each day the behavior is becoming more successful and thereby stronger; a professor who provides the same lecture year after year may or may not be aware of how student reactions have shaped his style and delivery into what it is; a couple in a long satisfying marriage may not be aware of how exquisitely sensitive and responsive to each other they have become. A reinforcement perspective has been used to account for almost every aspect of human activity, including language, literature, and creativity (Skinner, 1957); spirituality (Hayes, 1984); personality (Bolling et al., 2006); and intimacy and attachment (Kohlenberg, Kohlenberg, & Tsai, 2009a).

Taking awareness away from the process of reinforcement means that the primary way to determine if reinforcement has occurred is to observe future occurrences of the behavior. One may also refer to a non-behavioral system: the neurobiological changes that take place when reinforcement has occurred. Our bodies, however, do not have the appropriate sensory systems in the brain for detecting these subtle neurobiological changes when they occur. Synapses and pathways simply are strengthened. Certainly, sometimes in the moment, we may feel pleased and if asked, we might say we are likely to act this way again in the future. But this feeling is not reinforcement nor is it necessary to have this feeling in order to be reinforced.

Thus, reinforcement can be seen as an ongoing and ubiquitous process that does not exclude any aspect of human experience. Our clients' life problems can be viewed as the result of a history of contingencies of reinforcement, and psychotherapy can be seen as an opportunity to provide contingencies of reinforcement to enhance our clients' productive and fulfilling lives.

7

Natural versus arbitrary reinforcement

From a FAP perspective, behavioral change in any therapy results from the therapist consequating client behaviors. To achieve maximum potency, reinforcement must be contiguous (i.e., close in space and time to target behaviors), consistently and strategically scheduled, and natural rather than arbitrary. This last distinction is of critical importance in FAP as it influences the degree to which any change achieved within session may generalize to and be maintained in the outside environment. For this reason we would like to examine the distinction between natural and arbitrary reinforcement and how you might increase the use of natural reinforcement in session.

Distinguishing natural and arbitrary reinforcement

Arbitrary reinforcers are stimuli that have no direct or expected relationship in real life to the behaviors they follow (Kohlenberg & Tsai, 1991). To use a simple example, if a client is given candy each time s/he exhibits a target behavior of assertiveness in session, frequency of assertiveness may indeed increase in session, as long as candy is sufficiently appetitive and reinforcing to the client. The arbitrary reinforcer employed, however, candy in this case, has no direct or expected relationship to assertiveness. The presentation of candy after assertiveness requires intentional human mediation (on the part of the therapist) that would not be expected in daily life. The long-term problem, of course, is that any behavioral improvements that are shaped via these arbitrary reinforcers may not be maintained in the outside world where candies are not doled out for assertiveness. The over-use of arbitrary reinforcement eventually can lead to the emergence of two different repertoires—one shaped and maintained primarily within the therapy session consequated by these arbitrary reinforcers, and another maintained by very different contingencies in the outside world. This is not an effective therapeutic strategy when clients are most interested in changing their day-to-day lives and not just learning how to be good clients.

Natural reinforcers, on the other hand, *are* related to the consequences of behavior that occur in one's daily environment. They bear some inherent connection to the behavior at hand, such as feeling warm relates to putting on a coat or satisfying hunger relates to eating. Provided that the therapist's genuine reactions somewhat resemble those that the client is likely to encounter in the outside world (i.e., the therapist is a good representative of others with whom the client is likely to interact), the therapist's natural reinforcement of client improvements is not an artificial mediation.

What does this mean in practice? Using the same example discussed above, a naturally reinforcing response to client assertiveness might be compliance, willingness, or amenability on the part of the therapist, responses that are likely available in the client's daily life environment. Because these reinforcers are available both in therapy and the outside world, target behaviors (e.g., assertiveness) are more likely to generalize—that is, they are more likely to occur and be maintained in the client's outside life where they really matter.

Being naturally reinforcing in session

Because FAP therapists form genuine relationships with their clients from the earliest moments in therapy, over time they come to matter a great deal to their clients and can become powerful reinforcers for client change. More explicitly, this means that in time clients will notice and care about their therapists' responses and reactions, their impact on their therapists, and the dynamics in the therapeutic relationship that change as a result of their own behaviors. Although there are countless ways in which a therapist can be naturally reinforcing, typical therapist reinforcing responses include sharing, expressing, disclosing, or amplifying his or her reactions to client behavior. To be naturally reinforcing, therapists need to connect authentically with their clients just as people connect in the outside world. Therapists cannot be avoidant of the real intimacy that develops in a therapeutic relationship, nor the discomfort, strong feelings, and risk-taking that may be involved in the creation of a real relationship. Therapists are asked to be themselves as much as possible within the constraints of the therapy relationship in order to become more naturally reinforcing. At the same time, FAP therapists must balance their initial or reflexive responses to clients against more measured, strategic responses that take into consideration the function of clients' behavior. For example, if a client working on assertiveness finally speaks up and requests an early morning appointment (a functional improvement or CRB2, see Point 8), because of the strong, genuine, and caring bond the therapist feels towards the client, the therapist naturally is likely to comply even though coming in early is experienced as aversive. Similarly, if a conflict-avoidant client expresses displeasure about some aspect of the therapy for the first time (also a CRB2), the therapist's natural reaction is delight at the expression rather than defensiveness or frustration. The therapist is not overriding a natural punishing response in these situations; rather, because of the power of the therapeutic relationship and the true deep feelings of compassion and caring, the therapist is in fact being naturally and honestly reinforcing. Offering these natural reinforcers does not preclude genuineness related to the full range of the therapist's response. For example, the FAP therapist might say, "Although I'll be honest that I'm not a morning person, your assertiveness is really powerful and meaningful to me. Let's meet at 8 a.m. next week."

Although natural reinforcement typically reflects contingencies that exist in the client's outside environment, sometimes it is necessary to reinforce clients' successive approximations of target behaviors even if they are not quite skillful enough to be positively reinforced in the outside world. It is crucial that FAP therapists both recognize and reinforce these approximations in order to strengthen the target behavior so that it can be refined eventually to a skillful, effective level that would be naturally reinforced in daily life. In these cases, the therapist may make it clear to the client that the therapeutic relationship is in fact different from outside relationships, in that the therapist is more sensitive to client improvements than one can expect others to be. When the therapist feels that the client's behavior is "ready" for the outside world, this should be discussed.

8

Clinically relevant behaviors (CRBs)

At every moment during the therapy session, your clients are behaving. Some of these behaviors are obvious such as listening to you, making eye contact, talking, being silent, thinking about what they are going to say next, and expressing anger. Some behaviors are less obvious such as feeling (e.g., emotions like fear, sadness, love, worthlessness, rejection), perceiving (e.g., that you are concerned), interpreting, avoiding being in the moment, and emotionally withdrawing. If you can adopt the view that nearly everything a client does in session is behavior, then any particular moment in therapy opens up with possibility for you to be reinforcing. Out of the universe of possible behaviors to reinforce, we refer to a select subsample of behavior as clinically relevant behaviors (CRBs). They are called "clinically relevant" because they are the very same behaviors that occur in clients' daily lives that have brought them into therapy.

In some cases, CRBs are obvious. For example, a client who gets anxious and cannot think clearly when interacting with an authority figure has the very same problem with the therapist. In other cases, however, CRBs are identified functionally, and this is not at all obvious. For example, consider that a client's daily life relationship problems are the result of a tendency to inappropriately view love and caring expressed by a close partner as not being genuine (e.g., a "trust" issue). This client similarly thinks the therapist is expressing kindness and caring because s/he is "paid" to. Because of the difference between a close partner and a therapist, one might say these are not the same behaviors. But as expressed in Point 4, behavior is defined functionally, by context and meaning. In this case the behavior of interest is "trusting" others to be sincere and honest. From a functional standpoint, the trust behavior that occurs in the client's close relationship also occurs in the relationship with the therapist and thus is a CRB.

Some might recognize the resemblance between this notion of CRB and the psychoanalytic notion of transference where the patient transfers her or his neurosis to the therapist. To be sure, FAP posits that the client's daily life problems may occur in the context of the relationship with the therapist but, unlike psychoanalysis, CRBs are viewed as the result of normal, non-pathological stimulus generalization from daily life to the therapy relationship. In other words, in FAP, the client–therapist relationship is a real relationship.

There are three types of CRB, and understanding the distinction among these is central to doing FAP. CRB1s are client problems that occur in session. The trusting and speech anxiety examples given above are examples of CRB1s. To be clear, a client talking about trust or difficulties with authorities is not CRB. CRB1s actually occur in the here and now—"trusting problems" or "speaking anxiety problems" in relation to the therapist. CRB1s are by definition related to the client's presenting problems and often involve emotional avoidance such as not being open and difficulty expressing honest feelings or personal wants to the therapist. The daily life manifestations of these problems involve not being open, not asking for what one wants, and not honestly expressing feelings in relationships with intimate partners, parents, co-workers, and friends. An example would be a depressed individual who feels controlled by his wife and is passive in his relationship with her, and who shows up session after session with nothing to contribute to the therapy agenda, passively accepting whatever the therapist suggests.

CRB2s are client improvements that occur in session. Early in FAP, CRB2s do not occur or are quite weak (this would be expected since CRB1s are higher strength). A common theme for most therapists is to encourage clients to reveal innermost feelings that are typically avoided, such as fear, rejection, and love for the therapist. Not revealing, cutting oneself off from, or withholding these feelings from the therapist might be a commonly occurring CRB1. In those cases when emotional avoidance is a CRB1, expressing and having feelings about the therapy or therapist would be a CRB2. Similarly in those cases where the clients' daily life problem is not asking others for what they went, the CRB1 would be similarly not making requests of the therapist. Examples of parallel CRB2s might include asking for a reduced fee, requesting a change in the appointment time, or asking the therapist for a genuine impression about the client.

Note that the definition of CRB2 pivots on the word "improvement." In order to know whether a CRB2 has occurred, it is first important to know what the baseline CRB1 looks like. For example, consider the client who frequently and abruptly quits therapy without offering any explanation as to what precipitated this—a definite CRB1. After a number of CRB1 quits, this client for the first time told the therapist that she was quitting therapy because there was too long a period between therapy sessions. The therapist astutely recognized this latter quit as a CRB2 because an explanation was given, and reinforced the client by suggesting ways they could have shorter but more frequent visits.

CRB3s are client interpretations of behavior, which are frequent in session. Clients will often ask therapists for interpretations of their own behavior (e.g., "Why do I get so anxious when I try to assert myself?"). From a FAP standpoint, the preferred explanation is a more functional one that refers to histories of reinforcement and punishment. For example, if a client says "I get anxious because I don't believe I am a worthy person," the therapist might encourage a more functional interpretation such as "While growing up, whenever I attempted to assert myself or ask for what I wanted I was criticized, and thus punished, and, incidentally, I also felt worthless." The more functional interpretation is preferred because it points to a therapeutic solution, for example, "take a chance and ask for what you would like, and see if you get punished or not."

A failure to make the CRB1 versus CRB2 distinction can lead to counter-therapeutic interventions. Consider a therapist who was using CBT and relaxation to help a client overcome a fear of being assertive with her husband. After several weeks of this work, the therapist suggested they do a role-play in which the therapist would act out the role of the husband by demanding that the client iron his shirts and that she was then to practice role-playing assertiveness. The client politely refused to do the role-playing because it seemed too artificial to her. The therapist failed to recognize that this was a significant CRB2 of being assertive with the therapist (the desired goal for her and her husband) and told her she apparently did not fully understand the prior CBT and relaxation training, and so they would repeat this until she was more amenable to doing a role-play. No doubt the therapist had good intentions, but inadvertently missed a significant therapeutic opportunity, and even worse, punished a CRB2. The therapist's response was thus counter-therapeutic.

At the beginning of this point, we noted that the distinction between the types of CRBs is central to doing FAP. It is considered counter-therapeutic to inadvertently punish CRB2s and reinforce CRB1s. Effective FAP involves shaping, nurturing, and reinforcing CRB2s.

9

Emotions and feelings

Clients' emotions and feelings play a critical role in FAP. Our approach to this topic, however, is different from most other therapies. The difference in perspective is in (1) our explanation of what feelings are; (2) our assertion that feelings and emotions do not cause problematic behavior, but avoidance of them often does; and (3) our account of why it is important for our clients to be emotional during the therapy session.

In FAP, the term "feeling" is really two words, each with a distinct meaning. One meaning of feeling is as a verb, and the other is as a noun. When used as a verb, feeling is an activity, a type of sensory action, such as seeing or hearing. (Yes, to the behaviorist "seeing" is a behavior; it is something we do and is shaped by contingencies of reinforcement.) When it is a noun, a feeling (also referred to as an emotion) is the object that is felt as in "I feel (verb) a feeling (noun)."

What is the object being felt, however, when we feel depressed, anxious, happy, and hopeless? Our behavioral view asserts that what we feel is our body. The "interoceptive" and "proprioceptive" nervous systems are involved in the body feeling process. These two nervous systems are stimulated by the parts of the body involved in fear, anger, depression, anxiety, joy, and the like.

How does the body get in that particular state which is then felt? It is the result of our unique learning history (operant and respondent conditioning and associated verbal processes). The important point here is that we view the external environment as the ultimate cause of the bodily states associated with feelings such as fear, anger, hurt, and love. Just because the bodily state is present, however, does not mean one is aware of or can describe feelings.

We are not born knowing what our emotions are any more than

we are born knowing (or even noticing) what a ball is. These must be taught by adults, mainly our parents and caretakers. In the case of feelings, the object being felt (the body) is private and the parent or adult who is trying to teach a child to be aware of and identify feelings is at a disadvantage. In contrast to teaching the child to sense (see) a ball, the adult can point to the ball, pronounce its name, and reinforce a response such as "ball." Thus, it is not surprising there is confusion about what we feel. Nor is it surprising for a client to look puzzled and say "I don't know" when asked "what are you feeling right now?" In addition to being confused about labeling (or even being aware) of feelings, the expression or showing of feelings is often punished in our culture because we place substantial prohibitions on displays of emotion (Nichols & Efran, 1985). The net result is that many client problems involve difficulties due to: (1) identifying and/or describing feelings; (2) avoiding situations that evoke negative (or positive) feelings; and (3) not being aware of (cut off from) feelings or "numbing."

In the service of being aware of and evoking CRBs (Rules 1 and 2, see Point 18), you can offer your clients a behavioral rationale for getting in touch with feelings and for being emotional during the therapy session. FAP therapists underscore that the importance of being emotional in session is *not* based on the benefits of cathartic release (e.g., "It's good to get it out, to release those bottled up feelings," or "If you hold them back they will come out in some other way"). Instead, the rationale is that avoiding feelings has a cost. Avoiding feelings is accomplished through reduced awareness of one's own internal (bodily) states, one's external (interpersonal) environment, and deliberate avoidance of feeling evocative situations (e.g., keeping a distance from a potentially intimate relationship). Thus, the absence of emotion interferes with therapy, and correspondingly, with other areas of daily life. Emotional expression is crucial because it serves as a marker that clients are in touch with themselves and the world and provides them the opportunity to learn how to act in new ways that improve their lives. For example, we might say to a client who is avoiding grieving over a relationship that has ended:

"It's important to let yourself grieve, because if you avoid thinking, feeling, and talking about your ex, then you may end up avoiding those activities that you once did together, or meeting new people who might evoke the same feelings you had for your ex. Even worse, you might end up cutting off awareness of private feelings of attraction and connection. By avoiding all these things, not only is the richness of your life interfered with, but you also lose the opportunity to figure out what went wrong and to learn new ways of dealing with someone close to you when similar problems come up."

Another intervention that can help reduce emotional avoidance is to re-present, in the session, the situation that evokes the avoidance (CRB1). For example, when clients have difficulty accepting caring from others (the avoidance of expressions of caring feelings by others) and need help in getting in touch with and expressing their feelings, especially feelings of closeness, we encourage an active expression of feelings by therapists concerning their caring for and connection to the client.

In accordance with Rule 3 (see Point 18), a therapist's response to displays of emotion ideally should be naturally reinforcing to encourage reductions in emotional avoidance and to set the scene for therapeutic progress. A therapist who has difficulty with his/her own or with others' affective expression is unlikely to offer such encouragement and may inadvertently punish a client's contact with or expression of affect. Someone with this type of deficient repertoire clearly would be less able to work well with clients who require increased contact with stimuli evoking emotional responses. Therefore, therapists should strive to increase their awareness and be willing to work on dealing with their own issues. See Point 19 for questions that therapists can explore regarding their own avoidance repertoires so that they can more effectively help their clients address feelings.

10

Development of the self

Like emotions and feelings, the self figures prominently in many client presenting problems: "I have no self-esteem," "I don't know who I am," "I want to find my true self," or "My family says I have not been myself lately." The self, in fact, has been a salient topic in the history of psychotherapy, and many theories of the self have been advanced (Deikman, 1973; Erikson, 1968; Kohut, 1971; Masterson, 1985).

The reader might be surprised that behaviorists have something to say on this topic as well. To a behaviorist, experiencing or being aware of one's self is a behavior. But just as one may experience a good movie or the feeling of warm sun on the skin, one may experience or become aware of one's self.

What is the self? For many individuals, the self is that which has been present across all other experiences. What one thinks, sees, feels, wants, and so forth, will vary across time, but the experience of one's self is of something stable, a constant perspective from which thinking, seeing, feeling, and wanting occur. And like all behavior, experiencing one's self is learned. The nature of what is learned may vary depending on the quality of the instruction, just as what is learned about emotions and feelings may vary, as discussed in the last point. With the experience of the self and other private events, however, it turns out that the learning is quite tricky, and there is ample opportunity for problems to occur.

Consider a child learning to name a ball. When the child says "ball" in the presence of an actual ball, the parent or caregiver will demonstrate excitement or offer praise, providing reinforcement for the correct label. When the child says "ball" when the object referred to is not a ball, the parent will correct or ignore the child. In this way, over repeated instances of such training and through other behavioral processes beyond the scope of this example (Hayes, Barnes-Holmes, & Roche, 2001), the child learns to correctly identify balls. The training is relatively simple, because it is easy for parents to gauge whether the child is correct in saying "ball" by ascertaining that a ball is present.

Now consider a child learning to name "hunger." As with ball, we want the child to say "hunger" (or a functional equivalent, like "I want food," "food," "eat," or "hungry") in the presence of the experience of hunger and not in the presence of other experiences. The parental task here is undoubtedly more difficult than in the case of the ball. Hunger is much harder to identify because it is a private experience, not a public object to which the parent has easy visual or tactile access. The parent may notice the length of time since the child's last meal, how much the child has been eating lately, or the child's irritable mood and suggest, "You must be hungry." Sensitive parents of course successfully meet this challenge most of the time, but even the most attuned parents will not be as accurate with "hunger" as they will be with "ball."

Some parents unfortunately will not be very accurate at all with hunger or other private experiences. They may rely on the clock as the sole indicator of the child's mealtimes, disregarding the child's private experience of hunger altogether, or they may wait until they are hungry themselves before they consider the child's experience. Some may stifle the child's early attempts to name hunger with punishment for being irritable or crying. To a behaviorist, one's degree of accuracy and confidence with one's experience of hunger as an adult will be a function of these and other learning experiences, and should vary on a continuum from accurate and confident to inaccurate, confused and dependent on others based on the quality of the instruction. When asked if s/he is hungry, an adult with poor instruction in this regard may reply, "I don't know. Are you?" or say "no" even though hunger is present, not identifying the private experience. S/he may not notice hunger until food is present in the immediate context.

Many private experiences of clinical interest are like hunger. We must learn to identify and label our emotions, wants, needs, fantasies, memories, and so forth. The success with which we learn to do so has an impact on the success with which we learn to identify and experience our selves—the experience that is constant and present across all of these other experiences. Thus, one's experience of self may be accurate and confident, or inaccurate, confused, and dependent on others. Essentially, one may say with accuracy and confidence, "I know who I am," or one may say, "I don't know who I am." According to this theory, severe problems with the self, as in those experienced by clients diagnosed with borderline personality disorder or disorders of the self (e.g., dissociative identity disorder) are a function of severely disordered, neglectful, traumatic, and invalidating instruction with respect to private experiences (Kohlenberg & Tsai, 1991).

Thus, the FAP therapist sees no theoretical obstacles to working on problems of the self, and in fact employs a theoretical stance that may clarify the work to be done. Self-experiences may be conceptualized as varying on a continuum from complete private control over the experience (resulting in accurate and confident self-expressions) to complete public control (resulting in absent, inaccurate, confused, or dependent self-expressions). The therapeutic task is to shape private control over the experience, and functionally the therapeutic hour affords many opportunities to do so. Agenda setting, provision of homework, simple questions, even therapeutic misunderstandings, all may be seen as opportunities to evoke and reinforce client self-expression. In FAP, problems with the experience of self become CRB1s, and a full set of FAP techniques can be used to address and transform these issues (Kohlenberg, Tsai, Kanter, & Parker, 2009b).

11

Intimacy and attachment

Engaging in a satisfying intimate relationship is reported to be the most important source of happiness and well-being (Russell & Wells, 1994). A lack of ongoing interaction with close others is implicated in the onset, maintenance, and relapse of most clinical problems ranging from anxiety and mood disorders to substance abuse (Pielage, Luteijn, & Arrindell, 2005; Gable & Reis, 2006; Van Orden, Wingate, Gordon, & Joiner, 2005; Burman & Margolin, 1992). For this reason, helping our clients to create more intimacy in their lives comes near to reaching the status of a universal treatment goal.

As we define it, intimacy involves disclosure of one's innermost thoughts or feelings that results in a sense of connection, attachment, and close relationship with another. This sense of connection is an adult version of what Bowlby (1969) described in the relationship that develops between mothers and infants. Bowlby's fundamental hypothesis is that the contingencies of survival (natural selection) have thrust mothers and infants into each other's arms. In other words, powerful reinforcement existed for attachment behaviors such as clinging and turning toward primary caregivers in times of distress. Bowlby's hypothesis is consistent with FAP's behavioral hypothesis (Kohlenberg et al., 2009a; Mansfield & Cordova, 2007).

Needless to say, there are great individual differences in the ability to be open, to become attached, and, hence, to experience the sense of being connected to others. Although early studies of attachment tended to examine the process during childhood, more recently the focus has expanded to adult expressions of attachment, particularly in romantic and close relationships (Meyer & Pilkonis, 2001). Based on histories of contingencies experienced in being intimate, a wide range of attachment repertoires can influence people's propensity to engage in effective intimate relating. For example, the fear of rejection and its impacts on the development of close relationships are clear results of an individual's history of reinforcement and punishment with regard to intimate behavior. Attachment theorists have classified these behavioral repertoires in terms of "secure, anxious-ambivalent and anxious-avoidant attachment styles, which describe whether patients (and therapists) tend to be comfortable and confident in relationships, fearful of abandonment, or defensively separate" (Meyer & Pilkonis, 2001, p. 466). Meyer and Pilkonis's brief review of the literature concludes there are similarities among (1) the way children attached to caregivers, (2) how adults attach to romantic partners, and (3) how clients attach to their therapists. In other words, forming attachment relationships is functionally the same in these different contexts.

Intimacy in FAP includes inviting clients to be open and to reveal deeply held secrets of the heart and, even to become attached or dependent if this is a CRB2 for a particular client. This invitation sets the scene for evoking and then reinforcing improved intimate relating behaviors that constitute CRB2s. The "intimate relating" we are referring is labeled as "therapeutic intimate relating." This distinction is made since we believe that becoming attached, dependent, and turning to the therapist for help is topographically (but not functionally) different from the way these same patterns are exhibited in close relationships outside of therapy. The therapist is implicitly or explicitly requesting clients to take risks and to trust that they will not be punished.

Thus, from a FAP standpoint, the therapeutic relationship ideally would evoke client behavior that prevents intimacy from developing (CRB1s), and prompt and reinforce improvements in intimacy creating behaviors (CRB2s). According to Cordova and Scott (2001), becoming more intimate involves taking risks and is scary. The reason we fear attachment and connection is that we have been punished for such behaviors in the past (perhaps as far back as infancy). Thus, becoming more connected places us in an interpersonally vulnerable position. In the service of improving clients' emotionally intimate expressions, it is essential that therapists naturally reinforce interpersonally vulnerable behavior (CRB2s). In clients' daily lives, intimate expressions generally are reinforced by the other person's increased interest, focused attention, and reciprocal self-disclosures. Contrived or arbitrary responses such as "Thanks for sharing" probably would not be a natural reinforcer. Thus a client who discloses and expresses grief about the loss of someone close might best be served by a therapist who responds by revealing his or her deepest feelings of sadness about how to endure such a loss, along with willingness to hear the depths of such grief.

Not only do clients need to risk self-disclosing, they must also learn to reinforce the intimate interpersonal behavior of others in order to create and maintain close relationships. Thus the therapist's interpersonally vulnerable expressions must also be reinforced. Take the example of a therapist who expresses caring and concern about a client by disclosing that he thought about the client a great deal during the week. The client response, "That is what I pay you for," would punish such disclosures on the part of the therapist. This would be an opportunity for the therapist to point out a CRB1, that the client has blocked an opportunity to deepen the relationship. A CRB2 might be the client saying, "I am so moved, even a little frightened by the intensity of your caring for me. It is so new for me to have anyone care in this way, it even feels hard to trust it." In addition to reinforcing the connecting behavior of clients, there is another compelling reason for developing therapeutically intimate relationships. Sharpley (2010) has suggested that therapist–client attachment (à la Bowlby) is the common factor that underlies therapeutic alliance and is the non-specific factor responsible for improvement across all forms of psychotherapy. FAP therapists are committed to creating a compassionate, evocative, and reinforcing environment that can be described as a "sacred space" (see Point 15) in which clients learn to establish intimate relationships.

12

Cognitions and beliefs

As a behavioral therapy approach, how does FAP address cognitions and beliefs? As discussed in Point 2, many individuals without a behavioral background may have learned that behaviorists deny the existence of cognition and belief, that anything inside the "black box" of the mind that cannot be observed does not exist.

This characterization of behaviorism has no relation to FAP. FAP takes everything that a client does—acting, thinking, believing, loving, feeling, hoping, and so forth—seriously. Behaviorists do not deny mental experiences; they do eschew treating those experiences as entities to explain other experiences. For example, cognitive theory posits that cognitive structures such as schemas give rise to specific automatic thoughts as well as to overt behaviors (Clark, Beck, & Alford, 1999). While behaviorists argue that cognitive structures or schemas do not exist, they are very interested in the experience and process of thinking and in thoughts.

A trickier issue is whether thoughts cause behavior, and behaviorists over the years have been somewhat inconsistent on this issue. The first obstacle to viewing thoughts as causes was pragmatic in that traditionally, behaviorists preferred to locate causes in the environment, because environmental conditions are presumably manipulatable. Early behavioral interventions, however, sometimes included behavioral thought-stopping interventions, and modern cognitive therapists might reasonably argue that the techniques of cognitive therapy are quite effective at changing thoughts. Thus, the argument that thoughts are not manipulatable is not very convincing in today's psychotherapeutic environment.

The second argument against viewing thoughts as causes was theoretical. Because thinking is seen as a behavior, it is theoretically problematic for the behaviorist to suggest that one behavior (thinking) causes another behavior, as we want to look outside the behavioral system for causes of behavior. Both traditional behavioral accounts, however, of language and cognition (Skinner, 1957) and more recent accounts (Hayes et al., 2001) make it clear that thoughts, as private events, can have stimulus properties such as eliciting and evocative functions. In other words, what one thinks can influence how one feels and what one does. From a FAP perspective, any behaviorist who denies that thinking can have an impact on behavior is being unnecessarily dogmatic Thus, today's behaviorism includes rich and sophisticated accounts of language and cognition and how they influence overt behavior.

Equally dogmatic as the behaviorist who denies the role of cognition, from a FAP perspective, is a cognitivist who demands that all clinically relevant overt behavior must have cognitive causes. In FAP, sometimes thinking has an impact on behavior, and sometimes it does not (Kohlenberg, Kanter, Tsai, & Weeks, 2010). FAP, while allowing for the possibility that thinking may influence behavior, retains a behavioral worldview that explores the individual's historical and current context as the determinants of the relation between thinking and behavior. This suggests that whether thinking impacts behavior may vary from time to time depending on other contextual factors.

For example, consider a client with recurrent panic attacks. The client reports that the panic attack was triggered by getting on the bus, and when asked if s/he had any panic-related thoughts while getting on the bus, s/he reports "Yes, I remember thinking that I was trapped and that I could not easily get off the bus if I had to, and then very soon after that I started feeling panic." In this case, it is possible that the client's thinking was influential with respect to triggering the panic. Thus, the traditional cognitive A–B–C model, in which A represents an antecedent event (getting on the bus), B represents an intervening belief or cognition ("I feel trapped"), and C represents the emotional consequence (panic) would apply, and a FAP therapist might usefully employ this model as part of treatment.

Cognitive and FAP therapists would respond differently, however, if in response to the question about panic-related thoughts while getting on the bus, the client reported, "I was not aware of any. The panic just came on as soon as I sat down on the bus. Actually I was thinking about my work." A cognitive therapist dogmatically adhering to the A–B–C model possibly would continue to explore for automatic thoughts that occurred quickly in that situation and precipitated the panic, explaining that the thoughts may happen so fast that the client does not notice them, but upon reflection, they logically must be there. The FAP therapist would probably not do this, because our model allows for the possibility that the panic can be triggered directly by getting on the bus with no intervening thoughts.

Furthermore, there are other possibilities. For example, getting on the bus could cause both the panic-related thoughts and the panic symptoms simultaneously. In other words, the panic thoughts occurred, but they did not participate in causing the panic. Alternately, getting on the bus could directly cause the panic symptoms, then the symptoms caused the thoughts. This would be an A–C–B model (Kanter, Kohlenberg, & Loftus, 2004). The bottom line is that the behavioral worldview upon which FAP is based is very flexible, and sees the traditional A–B–C model as just one of many possible options for the relation between thinking and feeling.

Therapeutically, this opens up many interventions to the FAP therapist. When the A–B–C model applies, the techniques of Cognitive Therapy (e.g., Beck, Rush, Shaw, & Emery, 1979) may be used by FAP therapists to challenge thoughts. In fact, considerable theoretical and empirical work has been devoted to adding FAP techniques to those of Cognitive Therapy (CT), resulting in a treatment called FAP-Enhanced Cognitive Therapy, or FECT (R. J. Kohlenberg, Kanter, Bolling, Parker, & Tsai, 2002). In FECT, therapists assess on a situation by situation basis whether the A–B–C model applies. When it does, they employ cognitive techniques, although while doing so, as FAP therapists, they are alert to opportunities to shift into FAP processes when CRBs occur. More discussion of FECT is provided in Point 26 ("Openness to Techniques from Other Therapy Schools").

Even in cases where the A–B–C model applies, however, additional considerations may be useful before the FAP therapist engages in cognitive restructuring per se. First, even in cases when thoughts are causally related to clinically relevant behavior, behavioral research and theory (Hayes, Strosahl, & Wilson, 1999) suggest that challenging thoughts as per traditional cognitive therapy may not be the best or most useful approach (Longmore & Worrell, 2007). Instead, the FAP therapist may choose to help the client accept and defuse from the thoughts, rather than working directly at changing their content, as per the techniques of Acceptance and Commitment Therapy (ACT). Several published discussions and case studies of integrating FAP and ACT are available (Baruch, Kanter, Busch, & Juskiewicz, 2009a; Callaghan, Gregg, Marx, Kohlenberg, & Gifford, 2004; B. S. Kohlenberg & Callaghan, 2010).

Although FECT has been shown to be promising, ACT's acceptance-based approach to thoughts rather than CT's challenging approach ultimately may be a better fit with FAP and its worldview for several reasons. First, both ACT and FAP share a common foundation in behaviorism (although ACT has reframed and renamed this philosophy somewhat as *functional contextualism*). Second, in both ACT and FAP, the ultimate goal is behavior change in line with the client's stated goals and values, while CT takes a more medical symptom-reduction approach. Finally, the accepting stance of the ACT therapist dovetails nicely with the empathically connected approach of the FAP therapist, while the therapeutic relationship in CT is not as natural a fit with FAP. In fact, ACT techniques often focus the therapist on the here-and-now experience between the client and the therapist, affording easy opportunities to shift into FAP process while doing ACT.

13

Hidden meaning

If a woman says to her partner, "There is no more milk," what does she mean? Does she just mean there is no milk in the refrigerator? Or is she asking her partner to go to the store? Or is she irritated that her partner forgot to pick up the milk from the store as agreed? Similarly, if a client says, "I don't know what to do!", what does she mean? Is she just describing a state of confusion? Or might this be a prompt for the therapist to offer some suggestions?

For a behaviorist, the meaning of a statement is its function— what does the statement accomplish in the world? A behavior, including a statement that can be thought of as verbal behavior, may have functions of which we are not aware. For example, we may make the statement, "There is no more milk" unaware that we are requesting our partner to go to the store.

With verbal behavior (i.e., speaking, thinking, writing), the possibility of hidden functions (i.e., hidden meaning) is especially significant. Our clients sometimes say more with their words than is apparent. The behavioral notion of function provides a useful tool for unpacking this wisdom and systematically inquiring into the complexity of language (Kohlenberg & Tsai, 1991; Tsai et al., 2009c). In everyday life, we say that a verbal utterance has a surface or apparent meaning. For example, the above statement "There is no more milk," on the surface merely indicates that there is no milk in the refrigerator. We might evaluate the truth of this statement and a conventional analysis of the meaning of the statement might stop there. A full behavior analysis, however, would evaluate the context in which the statement was made to address the question, "What function did the statement serve?" For the behavior analyst, the meaning of an utterance extends beyond its apparent meaning to its function. Even if it is true that there is no more milk, there are additional questions to answer: Why was it said now and not earlier or later? Where was it said? What happened right after it was said? What happened earlier in the histories of the speaker and listener relevant to this event? Thus, an entire narrative is wrapped around the single statement, "There is no more milk." We might imagine numerous stories in which the same statement occurs.

Just as the same utterance may occur in multiple different stories, it may serve a range of functions besides the most obvious. Daily life is, of course, full of examples of statements with obvious hidden meanings, such as when a teenager says sarcastically, "Wow, thank you for enlightening me!" or a neighbor, panting as he lifts a dresser up his front steps, comments, "Man, this is really heavy." These hidden meanings, as noted, are relatively obvious and both speaker and listener are aware of the multiple meanings.

A crucial point for the FAP therapist to keep in mind, however, is that hidden meanings of therapeutic interest *may not be deliberate or conscious*. The client who when confused says, "I don't know what to do!" and stares plaintively at her therapist while her mind goes blank and panic crawls up her belly may not be aware that repeatedly when she has shared confusion with important others in the past, they have jumped into action for her. Thus, she now favors sharing confusion (and feels increasingly anxious until the other acts) over a range of other possible responses. That is, her statement functions as an indirect or non-deliberate request that the other person act for her. This example can be compared directly to the idea that some suicidal threats, while ostensibly intended to inform the listener of intentions to engage in self-harm, may be covert or hidden cries for help or attention. The function is obtained from the history in that this was the only way that this person had received such help (reinforcement) from family and caregivers in the past, and s/he may or may not have conscious awareness of the function or insight into the history that supplied it.

In another common form of hidden meaning, the presence of an aversive situation that a client does not wish to address directly prompts the client to mention a different (possibly less aversive) but related topic. For example, when the end of therapy with a cherished therapist approaches, a client may increasingly talk about unrelated losses and goodbyes; or, a client who is dissatisfied with her progress in therapy may talk at length about her frustration at being unable to clean up her garage.

The therapeutic value of exploring hidden meaning includes discovering CRBs. For example, a suicidal threat that is really a problematic bid for being listened to or receiving empathy (CRB1) might be shaped into more effective direct behavior that serves the same function (e.g., asking the therapist for more time or evidence of caring). Similarly, the client who talks about having difficulty cleaning up the garage may be avoiding (a CRB1) directly expressing feelings (likely a CRB2) about being dissatisfied with progress in therapy. In more general terms, exploring hidden meanings resembles the psychoanalytic goal for making the unconscious conscious but, in FAP, it emphasizes using this new awareness to improve interpersonal relating.

Hidden meanings, like other possible CRBs and any functional analysis, should be assessed gently and with an open mind. In exploring potential hidden functions of a client statement, the following questions might be kept in mind. We are not suggesting these questions be asked directly of clients, but that they may be helpful when clients are astute and the therapeutic alliance is strong:

- How have others responded to such statements in the past?
- How might such statements have been reinforced or shaped?
- Is there a hidden request?
- In what situations does such a statement occur?
- What other similar topics might be on the client's mind?
- What themes are raised by this statement?
- Is there an elephant in the room? Might this statement be related to the elephant?

Because of the power such hidden functions may have in a client's relationships, it is important that FAP therapists practice becoming aware of potential hidden meanings in their clients' speech, as well as in their own.

14

The therapy relationship is a real relationship

The foundation on which FAP rests is that the client–therapist relationship has the potential to evoke actual instances of clients' problematic daily life behaviors. For example, consider clients who try to please important others and do this at the expense of not asking for and not creating the possibility of receiving what is vital to them. FAP is based on the assumption that such clients will have the opportunity to do the same thing in the context of the therapist–client relationship. That is, they will do everything they can to please the therapist and not ask the therapist to meet some of their expectations and needs. In FAP terminology, the client's "not asking" is referred to as CRB1 (see Point 8), an actual here-and-now, in vivo occurrence of the daily life problem. Once the therapist becomes aware that this CRB1 is occurring, the therapeutic work is straightforward: it is to nurture, shape, and strengthen improved in vivo client behavior (CRB2). For example, the goal would be to strengthen or naturally reinforce the client's ability to take risks along with being more direct and skillful in expressing what s/he wants from the therapist and therapy. The goal of therapy is accomplished when the client's improved interpersonal skills developed in the therapeutic relationship generalize to daily life relationships.

The preceding gives rise to the following question: "Given that the therapy environment and the therapist are so obviously different from the kind of relationships and people that exist in the client's daily life, how is it possible for the client's daily life problems to occur during therapy? Correspondingly, if there are improvements within the therapist–client relationship, why would they be expected to generalize to daily life? Implied in the above question is the idea that the therapy relationship is an artificial one, and is differentiated from the "real" relationships that exist in the outside world.

We acknowledge that many features of the therapy situation are artificial, for example, meeting once a week at a specific time for 45 minutes, fee for service, boundaries such as not having outside the therapy room contact with clients, and prohibitions against physical intimacy. On the other hand, if we use our behavioral lens to examine what actually is "real" about the therapy relationship, we turn to functional analysis to understand the meaning of the term "real." What is "real" in the therapy relationship is defined as that which evokes the same responses that are evoked in daily life relationships—that is, the situations are functionally the same. For example, the typical therapy setting is defined by two people who come together to talk about the problems of one of the discussants. By its very nature, the therapy setting is an interpersonal context that requires risk-taking, disclosure, trust, and honesty; therefore it contains all of the stimuli associated with evaluation, rejection, and social punishment in addition to the stimuli associated with the emotional closeness of being attended to and cared about. Similarly, therapy relationships have beginnings and endings. Thus, if the client's daily life issues have to do with intimacy, risk-taking, disclosure, trust, rejection, beginnings and endings (as they often do, see Point 11) and these issues are evoked in the therapist–client relationship, functional analysis would indicate that the therapy relationship is "real" in these domains. By the same token, if the therapy relationship is functionally the same in this way, generalization would be expected to occur.

Clients sometimes will say they cannot emotionally connect, be open, vulnerable, or be therapeutically intimate with the therapist (see Point 11) due to the artificial boundaries such as the common limits regarding time and frequency of sessions. Although this might be a valid objection, it is important for the FAP therapist to maintain a functional perspective. For example, if the client's daily life problem has to do with forming intimate relationships, the functional similarity (reality) between therapy and outside relationships is that all relationships (both inside and outside of therapy) have limitations and boundaries. The client's CRBs might include not taking the risks that are necessary to connect and to deal with the limitations and disappointments inherent in all relationships.

We have focused here on how to apply functional analysis to account for and assess those areas in which the therapy relationship is real (i.e., the "same" as daily life). We should also point out that FAP includes interventions and suggestions as to how to enhance the functional equivalence or the reality of the therapist–client relationship. FAP therapists are encouraged (in the therapy context with their clients' target behaviors in mind) to be their real selves, to self-disclose, to be genuine, to express positive feelings, and to be courageous and therapeutically loving both in evoking and in naturally reinforcing client behavior (Points 22, 23, and 24). Similarly, FAP therapists generally eschew using standardized "one size fits all" interventions and limit the use of role-playing, behavioral rehearsal, or social skills training because these methods pose the risk of being artificial and might decrease functional equivalence (realness). Furthermore, once CRB2s take place in the therapy relationship, FAP offers guidance (see Points 23 and 25) in helping to transfer gains from the therapist–client relationship to the client's daily life.

15

Creating a sacred space of trust and safety

The importance of fostering trust and safety cannot be overstated in FAP. The therapist may choose to describe this process as "creating a sacred space" for therapeutic work. According to the *Oxford Dictionary*, a sacred space is dedicated, set apart, exclusively appropriated to some person or special purpose, and is protected by sanction from injury or incursion. Use of this term with clients may be quite powerful. Whether or not a FAP therapist chooses to use the term "sacred space" with clients, the key issue is that, functionally, the relationship is indeed sacred as defined here, and creating trust and safety is essential.

Trust, behaviorally speaking, may be seen as a predisposition to approach another person in a situation in which one could potentially get hurt. Thus, trust essentially describes a situation in which one person is predisposed to take risks in the presence of, and toward, another person. Instilling trust and safety are crucial in FAP because clients are shaped and reinforced to take risks, to be vulnerable, to push beyond their boundaries of comfort, and to take more steps to trust the therapist. That said, the behavior of trusting may be a goal of therapy and it is the rare client who will trust fully from the first session. Indeed, such blind trust may be as problematic as an inability to trust.

Fostering a sense of trust and safety, as everything else in FAP, is an idiographic process. Thus, for many clients, a host of what have been referred to as "non-specific" behaviors, such as accurate empathy, warmth, reflective listening, and validation, may be very important early therapist behaviors toward this end.

Although many theorists, particularly Carl Rogers (1961), argue that the important quality of such non-specific therapist responses is that they are unconditional (not contingent on particular client responses), the FAP therapist takes a different stance. As described more fully by Follette, Naugle, and Callaghan (1996), the FAP therapist's responses are seen as potentially reinforcing broad classes of behaviors (e.g., trusting and other therapy-facilitating and relationship-building behaviors). The therapist's behaviors are seen as generalized contingent reinforcement for the class of behaviors necessary for therapy to occur and a relationship to develop. This class includes behaviors like trusting, showing up on time, disclosing important personal information, paying attention and responding appropriately to questions, demonstrating caring and concern for the therapist's feelings, and being engaged in-session.

For the typical FAP client, however, fostering trust and safety may move beyond these basic therapy skills and into areas that are much more personal and genuine. Therapists can foster a sense of trust and safety with these clients by being more forthcoming with their thoughts, reactions, and observations (not hiding behind a therapist persona). And they can encourage clients: (1) to ask questions (e.g., "What are your questions about me, my training, my background?" or "What qualities do you most seek in a therapist?"); (2) to voice their reactions to the therapist (e.g., "What reactions do you have to my gender, age, ethnicity?"); and (3) to voice their feelings related to the appointment (e.g., "What are your thoughts and feelings about having this appointment today?" or "What would make this a really good first session for you?"). The FAP therapist, however, remains open to the possibility that some therapist behaviors may be aversive to specific clients depending on their histories, so assessment of the therapist's stimulus functions is important from the very beginning of therapy.

Numerous behaviors can help to engender another's trust. These trust-building behaviors are not specific to the therapy situation. In FAP we do not believe the therapist becomes a different person when stepping into a therapy room. Rather, behaviors that are well practiced and integrated outside therapy are more likely to succeed in the therapy room. These trust-enhancing behaviors may include: (1) providing accurate empathic reflections; (2) being honest and genuine; (3) keeping one's word; (4) being consistent and predictable, or explaining why one is being inconsistent and unpredictable so that the behavior makes sense; (5) recognizing another's expectations, and correcting them if not accurate, or explaining why one is not meeting them; (6) admitting when one does not know the answer; (7) seeing what is in someone's best interest and not taking advantage of or hurting him or her; (8) remembering the important things someone has revealed—people, events, memories; (9) being willing to match the other person's vulnerability; (10) being able to admit and take responsibility for mistakes, to repair ruptures; and (11) treating client truths and disclosures with care and reverence.

In the service of client growth, we not only shape our clients' behavior, but allow ourselves in turn to be shaped by our clients. As Martin Buber (n.d.) stated, "All journeys have secret destinations of which the traveler is unaware." Allow yourself to experience each therapeutic relationship as within sacred space on such a journey.

Part 2

THE DISTINCTIVE PRACTICAL FEATURES OF FAP

16

The treatment rationale and the beginning of therapy

The therapy rationale is a discussion that takes place with clients at the beginning of treatment. It offers an explanation of the possible causes of the presenting problems as well as a description of what the treatment will be like. The rationale is important because it helps to set the context for the types of intervention used in FAP and moderates therapeutic alliance issues that can be brought about by disparate expectations between client and therapist. For this reason we recommend formally presenting a rationale, whether written or verbal. If no rationale statement is made, the client draws on past experience or common knowledge about what any treatment will entail, and if that picture is different from the therapist's plan, it may impede progress.

Other than affirming that therapist–client relationship is both a focus and a key factor in achieving treatment goals, there is no one size fits all FAP rationale. The examples below contain a range of FAP rationales that illustrate: (1) ways therapists may adapt their rationales to fit their therapy approaches; (2) therapy parameters (e.g., brief or longer term); (3) treatment goals; and (4) the amount of risk taken by the therapist in terms of how evocative the rationale is. Frequently, even mentioning that there will be a focus on the therapist–client relationship might be evocative of CRB.

Example 1: Rationale given in the second therapy session

The following stated rationale and the client's reaction to it took place during the second treatment session. In the first session, the client reported that her primary problems included unhappiness, low self-esteem, a sense that she was not a good person, and the belief that others, especially her mother, generally thought poorly of her. During the second session, the following rationale was presented after focussing on the client's perceptions of the therapist's reaction to her:

Therapist: You'll notice I've talked a lot about the two of us, and I want to tell you why. I think that one of the most powerful ways for therapy to be effective is to actually work on your problems as they are occurring, so, for example, if you're upset about your mother or having difficulty relating to your mother, we might sit here and talk about it. That might be helpful. We can figure out how you feel and how she feels and so on, and we'll do some of that. But it's more powerful if the problems you're having you actually experience in the relationship with me. So, for example, you did. That is, you reacted to what happened at the end of the last session very much in the same way that's modeled after your reaction to Mom.

Client: Right.

Therapist: The therapy is just more powerful and effective if you can actually grasp on these things while they're occurring. So I wanted to let you know why I've been asking you these questions and focusing on our relationship.

Example 2: Excerpt from a highly evocative written rationale

What You May Expect in Our Therapy Work Together:
Clients come into therapy with complex life stories of joy and anguish, dreams and hopes, passions and vulnerabilities, unique gifts and abilities. Your therapy with me will be conducted in an atmosphere of caring, respect and commitment in which new ways of approaching life are learned. Our work will be a joint effort; your input is valued and will be used in the treatment plan and in weekly homework

assignments. I will be investing a great deal of care and effort into our work together, and I expect you to do the same. I will be checking with you in an ongoing way about what is working well for you in our relationship and what needs to be changed.

The type of therapy that I will be doing is called Functional Analytic Psychotherapy (FAP). It is a therapy developed at the University of Washington that is behaviorally based, but has the theoretical foundation to incorporate methods from other therapeutic modalities when appropriate. FAP emphasizes that the bond that will be formed between you and me will be a major vehicle in your healing and transformation.

The most fulfilled people are in touch with themselves and are able to be interpersonally effective. They are able to speak and act compassionately on their truths and gift, and are able to fully give and receive love. FAP will focus on bringing forth your best self. In order to do that, you must first be in touch with yourself at a core level (e.g., needs, feelings, longings, fears, values, dreams, missions). You will have the opportunity to learn how to express yourself fully, to grieve losses, to develop mindfulness, and to create better relationships. All aspects of your experience will be addressed, including mind, body, feelings, and spirit. I will be challenging you to be more open, vulnerable, aware and present. There is an optimal level of risk-taking in any situation, however, and it's important that you and I monitor how much outside your comfort zone to be is best for you at any given time.

It will be important for us to focus on our interaction if you have issues (positive or negative) or difficulties that come up with me which also come up with other people in your life. When one feels the power in expressing one's thoughts, feelings, and desires in an authentic, caring and assertive way, one has a greater sense of mastery in life. Our therapeutic relationship will be an ideal place for you to practice being powerful.

I consider the space that you enter with me in therapy to be sacred—I am privileged to be embarking on a journey of exploration and growth with you, and I will hold all that you share with reverence and with care. I will be a genuine person in the room with you, and my main guiding principle is to do that which is in your best interest.

Example 3: Excerpt from a less evocative version of the above

FAP often includes the empirically supported Cognitive Behavior Therapy protocols for specific disorders. At the same time, FAP emphasizes that the therapist–client relationship is important for accomplishing significant life change. Thus in addition to a specific symptom focus as needed, FAP also provides the opportunity to bring forth your best self, to learn how to express yourself fully, to grieve losses as needed, to develop mindfulness, and to create better relationships.

It will be important for us to focus on our interaction if you have issues (positive or negative) or difficulties that come up with me which also come up with other people in your life. Our therapeutic relationship will be an ideal place for you to practice being more effective in your relationships with others.

Example 4: Rationale given in a FAP-informed brief treatment study

Therapist: This study is about helping you to increase feelings of closeness and respect in your relationship. Contrary to a lot of other therapies that focus on telling you how to do things, the way we will try to help you increase your ability to have closeness is to actually practice it between you and me. Research shows that really effective therapists tend to think about how what is showing up here between you and me in the therapy room is showing up in your relationship. For example, for your goal of wanting to be more thoughtful in your relationship, we then ask how can thoughtfulness occur in here, between us? How do we know that you're actually working on being a thoughtful person here, in this brand new relationship with me? That's the premise of this sort of work and what we will be dealing with.

Client: So if I may ask, is the idea that this is a study to try to validate that enacting some of the behavioral changes here that we're wanting to manifest in the primary relationship can happen more readily if you practice it specifically in our therapeutic relationship?

Therapist: Yes, and it's not role-playing. It's actually much more powerful when it's real and happening between us, and I can give you a really authentic and genuine feedback. For example, you were being thoughtful in the way that you asked about and tried to understand what I was doing. It made me feel more comfortable with you and it sounded like you actually cared.

The above examples illustrate the primary theme present in FAP: a focus on the therapist–client relationship as a real relationship that plays a central role in the change process. In each case, the FAP rationale is the therapist's personal invitation to the client to participate in a meaningful interpersonal relationship.

17

Assessment and flexible case conceptualization

Many FAP therapists may start treatment focused on diagnostic assessment. Such an assessment can be helpful and may lead the therapist to choose specific empirically supported intervention strategies to administer while looking for opportunities to move into FAP process. For example, a clinician may choose to conduct ACT (Hayes et al., 1999), Cognitive Therapy (Beck et al., 1979), or Behavioral Activation (Martell, Dimidjian, & Herman-Dunn, 2010), and use case conceptualization frameworks developed for those treatments. To supplement those conceptualizations, a FAP conceptualization can identify when treatment targets may appear in the therapy room. For example, if conducting ACT, what will fusion or experiential avoidance look like in session? If conducting Cognitive Therapy, what types of cognitive distortions will the client make about the therapist? When conducting Behavioral Activation, will the client demonstrate passivity, avoidance of intimacy, and lack of action with respect to the therapy relationship?

Whether in the context of another treatment or not, FAP case conceptualization moves beyond diagnostic assessment and focuses on idiographically identifying and defining CRBs in such a way that maximizes the possibility that the therapist will observe, evoke, and reinforce them in session. The therapist's goal is to understand the client's interpersonal behavioral repertoires—how they function in the client's daily life, and how they function in the therapy room. There is no correct way to do this in FAP, but in general we distinguish between attempts to assess in-session behaviors and out-of-session behaviors.

Regarding assessment of in-session behaviors, Rule 1 of FAP (described in Point 19) is always in effect: no matter what the therapist is doing, he or she is always sensitive to the possibility that CRB may be occurring. Simply paying attention to CRBs should make it more likely that the therapist will respond appropriately and immediately when they occur.

In terms of out-of-session behaviors, many FAP therapists will engage in an informal assessment that is probably similar to what other therapists do—they ask about the client's presenting problems and goals, and learn about the details of the client's life via self-report. As described by Kanter et al. (2009), some FAP therapists may choose to use behavioral terminology in their case conceptualizations, while others may use more standard cognitive-behavioral or mainstream language. Some FAP therapists may also employ a variety of collaborative strategies to identify the client's goals and values, develop an appreciation for the salient aspects of the client's history, and begin to identify CRBs. These strategies include goals and values assessments, similar to those of ACT, mission statements, and homework assignments to write brief autobiographies summarizing milestones and losses. Some therapists choose to add a formal assessment strategy developed to identify behavioral repertoire problems in FAP, the Functional Idiographic Assessment Template (FIAT; Callaghan, 2006a), which is described more fully in Point 19.

Whatever the method, the important issue is that the FAP therapist is trying to identify clinically relevant interpersonal operant behaviors that occur both in the client's daily life and in the therapy room—CRBs. It is essential that these behaviors are defined as *functional classes*, or sets of behaviors that are defined by similar antecedents and consequences, rather than by similar forms. For example, a quintessential CRB1 in FAP is avoidance of genuine intimate expression. To understand this as a functional class, we would seek to understand what sorts of contexts trigger the behavior and what sorts of consequences follow it. Essentially, when faced with the opportunity to express genuine intimacy, the client escapes or avoids the situation, thereby avoiding feared negative consequences. This avoidance may look very different from situation to situation. In one context, it may take the form of literal flight, while in another, the client may stay in the situation but make jokes or express hostility. All of these behaviors would be considered in the same functional class in FAP.

A FAP case conceptualization form used by many FAP therapists includes the following categories (see Appendix, Tsai et al., 2009c): relevant history, daily life problems, variables maintaining problems, assets, and strengths, CRB1s, CRB2s, daily life goals, planned interventions, T1s (therapist in-session problems), and T2s (therapist in-session target behaviors). A simplified version of this form also can be used, where the initial task of the therapist is to learn about the client's daily life problems and goals for therapy and then to speculate about what instantiations of those problems and improvements might look like in the therapy relationship. For example, a client identified as a problem her difficulty in saying "no" to people when it was appropriate to do so, with the parallel goal of improving her ability to say "no" when appropriate. The therapist speculated that issues of compliance and "therapist-pleasing" might show up in therapy as CRB1, and that saying "no" to the therapist and demonstrating non-compliance at times with therapist requests would be CRB2. The therapist discussed and refined these hypotheses with the client over time. A therapist may find this case conceptualization somewhat redundant, in that the in-session goals and daily life goals are very similarly written. The direct parallel, however, is in fact useful and should simplify the issue—sometimes, after all, the best therapy does not have to be too complicated.

18

Use of therapeutic rules

Doing FAP entails implementing five therapeutic rules that shift the focus of treatment to clinically relevant behaviors (CRBs, see Point 8). Rather than the rigid quality associated with common usage of the term "rule," FAP rules are suggestions for therapist behavior that typically lead to positive client change and thus reinforce the therapist. Although the rules are delineated clearly here for instructional purposes, in practice they join together, and interventions typically encompass several rules simultaneously. FAP rules can facilitate therapists in taking advantage of therapeutic opportunities that may otherwise go unnoticed (Tsai, Kohlenberg, Kanter, & Waltz, 2009d).

Rule 1: Watch for CRBs (Be aware)

This rule is the core of FAP and its implementation can lead to a more intense and interpersonally oriented treatment. The more frequently that therapists detect and respond therapeutically to CRBs, the more likely it is that therapy will be effective, fascinating, and profound.

Rule 2: Evoke CRBs (Be courageous)

From a FAP standpoint, the ideal client–therapist relationship evokes CRB1s, which in turn are the precursors for the development and nurturing of CRB2s. Since CRBs are idiographic or pertain to the unique circumstances and histories of individual clients, the ideal therapeutic relationship will depend on what a particular client's daily life problems happen to be. If a client is anxious, depressed, or has difficulty committing to a course of action, then almost any type of psychotherapy has the potential to evoke relevant CRBs. FAP, however, also focuses on relationship and intimacy issues such as deeply trusting others, taking interpersonal risks, being authentic, and giving and receiving love. Thus, FAP calls for therapists to be present and to structure their therapy in a way not typically found in other behavior therapies. See Point 20 for a discussion of how therapists can strive to be more courageous in ways that evoke and reinforce client target behaviors.

Rule 3: Reinforce CRB2s naturally (Be therapeutically loving)

Rule 3 is somewhat enigmatic in that FAP is based on the assertion that reinforcement is the primary mechanism of change, yet deliberate efforts to reinforce run the risk of producing contrived or arbitrary rather than natural reinforcement. As discussed in Point 7, arbitrary reinforcement might strengthen "good" client behavior that is suitable for therapy sessions but will not generalize or be useful in daily life. Even worse, arbitrary reinforcement might be seen by the client as manipulative and thus jeopardize trust-building. Pre-planned therapist reinforcers such as saying "that's fantastic" or smiling are likely to be arbitrary. Instead, natural reinforcement is facilitated by a genuine caring about clients and their development of behavior that will improve their lives and interpersonal relationships.

The therapist who is aware of the occurrence of CRB2s and sees them as stepping stones to client goals, is in turn, likely to respond in a naturally reinforcing manner that will help clients generalize improvements to daily life. One way we describe the therapist frame that leads to being naturally reinforcing is to be therapeutically loving. Our behavioral definition of therapeutic love is that the therapist is willing to take steps, within the boundaries of the therapeutic relationship, that will best serve the client's interests. For further discussion of "therapeutic love" see Point 21.

Rule 4: Observe the potentially reinforcing effects of therapist behavior in relation to CRBs (Be aware of one's impact)

Rule 4 highlights the importance of paying attention to changes in client target behavior and the relationship between these changes and the therapist's contingent responding (e.g., reinforcement). By definition, the client has experienced reinforcement only if s/he exhibits the target behavior with increased frequency, intensity, or both. Thus, the only way a therapist truly knows that a response that was intended to be reinforcing actually was reinforcing is by observing a change in the frequency or intensity of the target behavior. Explicit process questions, however, also can serve to give the therapist clues about the reinforcing effects of his or her responses. These questions can be fairly straightforward and often occur after a CRB2/Rule 3 interaction. For example, the therapist may simply ask, "How was that for you?" or "How did you feel when I said just now that I am inspired by your risk-taking this week?" or "Do you think my response made it more likely for you to do what you did again, or less likely?"

An important consideration when asking these questions is the timing. Although they should follow therapist attempts to reinforce CRB, they probably should not follow too closely. A CRB2/Rule 3 interaction in FAP may be quite intense. Immediate attempts to "process" this interaction with Rule 4 type questions may truncate the natural interaction and may in fact represent a therapist's subtle avoidance of the intensity created. Thus, the therapist should be sensitive to the natural end to a CRB2 interaction and only follow with Rule 4 when the interaction has come to a natural end. This may result in the therapist waiting until the next session to process the interaction.

In terms of Rule 4, it is also important for therapists to focus on the role of what we refer to as T1s (therapist in-session problem behaviors) and T2s (therapist in-session target behaviors) (see Point 19) because an increased awareness of oneself corresponds with an increased awareness of one's impact on clients.

Rule 5: Provide functional analytically informed interpretations and implement generalization strategies (Interpret and generalize)

A functional analytically informed interpretation includes a history that accounts for how it was adaptive for clients to act in the ways they did and how to generalize progress in therapy to daily life. Implementing Rule 5 emphasizes "out-to-in parallels" when daily life events correspond to in-session situations and "in-to-out parallels" when in-session improvements correspond to daily life events. Both are important, and a good FAP session may involve considerable weaving between daily life and in-session content through multiple in-to-out and out-to-in parallels. One example involves a client pulling away from her therapist expressing caring (out-to-in parallel), and then relaxing into this caring and allowing it to happen in her daily life (in-to-out parallel).

Facilitating generalization is essential in FAP; success has not been achieved unless clients change their behavior in daily life. Thus, provision of homework is also important to Rule 5. The best homework assignments are made when a client has engaged in a CRB2 and the assignment is for the client to then take the improved behavior "on the road" (see Point 23) and test it with significant others.

19

Awareness (Rule 1, Rule 4)

Being aware of clients' CRBs as they are occurring is central to creating a more intense, effective, and interpersonally oriented treatment. Awareness leads to better, more accurate detection of and therapeutic responses to CRBs, resulting in a more profound therapy experience. Being aware can have a marked effect on how therapists see their clients, the case conceptualization, and the focus of treatment.

Therapists can sharpen their ability to detect CRBs in a number of ways.

A   **Be aware of therapeutic situations that frequently evoke CRBs.** Situations that often evoke CRBs include time structure (i.e., 45–50 minute hour), fees, and/or therapist characteristics (e.g., age, gender, race, and attractiveness). Others might be a silence in the conversation, a client's expression of affect, a client doing well, a therapist providing positive feedback or expressions of caring, and/or a client feeling close to the therapist. Still others could be a therapist's vacations, mistakes, or unintentional behavior; unusual events (e.g., a client seeing the therapist with a partner outside of therapy, the therapist becoming pregnant), and/or therapy termination. When circumstances like these occur, being aware of possible CRBs and probing for client reactions can lead to more productive therapy.

B   **Use your own reactions as a barometer.** A therapist's personal reactions to a client can be a valuable sensor for CRBs. Questions you can ask yourself include: What are the ways your client has a negative impact on you? Does your attention wander because s/he talks tangentially? Is s/he avoidant of your questions? Does s/he frustrate you because s/he procrastinates on homework assignments? Does s/he say one thing and do another? Is s/he critical of your every intervention? Does s/he pull away when the two of you have had a close interaction? Does s/he seem to have no interest or curiosity in you as a person? A key issue is knowing when your responses to a client are representative of how others in the client's life might respond, and when your responses are idiosyncratic. To the degree your responses are representative, they are a good indicator that CRB may be occurring.

C   **Identify possible CRBs based on FIAT-Q (Functional Idiographic Assessment Template) responses.** Numerous CRBs can be detected based on the five response classes in the FIAT-Q (Callaghan, 2006a) that are associated with interpersonal effectiveness:

1   *Class A:* Assertion of needs (identification and expression). The term "needs" stands for anything that one wants or values, including the need to state who one is, opinions, ideas, wishes, passions, longings, and dreams. Possible CRB1s include difficulty identifying or expressing what one needs from the therapist or being too demanding, feeling too vulnerable when receiving help, or unable to tolerate the therapist saying no to requests.

2   *Class B:* Bi-directional communication (impact and feedback). This class of behaviors involves how one gives and responds to feedback, both verbal and non-verbal. Possible CRB1s include difficulty receiving and providing either appreciations or constructive criticism, unreasonable expectations of self or therapist, little awareness of or hypersensitivity to impact on therapist, talking too long or too tangentially without checking impact, being too quiet, holding too much or too little eye contact, and exhibiting body language that does not match verbal content.

3   *Class C:* Conflict. The term "conflict" refers to having disagreement or an uncomfortable interaction. Possible CRB1s include inability to tolerate conflict or disagreement, being

conflict avoidant or engaging in conflict as a way to avoid closeness, expressing too much anger, being ineffective at resolving conflict, assuming too much self-blame or blaming therapist for problems, and expressing anger indirectly (e.g., by being passive-aggressive).

4   *Class D:* Disclosure and interpersonal closeness. This class of behaviors involves one's feelings about closeness, how one self-discloses about one's experiences, feels understood by others, and appreciates others and their needs. Possible CRB1s include having difficulty expressing or receiving closeness and caring, being reluctant to self-disclose or take emotional risks, talking too much about self, not listening well, not being aware of therapist's needs (e.g., going overtime, not giving therapist the opportunity to talk), and having difficulty trusting.

5   *Class E:* Emotional experience and expression. The term "emotional experience" refers to all types of emotions, both negative (e.g., sadness, anxiety, loneliness, anger) and positive (e.g., love, pride, joy, humor). Possible CRB1s include difficulty identifying, feeling, and expressing negative or positive feelings, expressing feelings in an overly intense manner, and avoiding emotional expression and experience.

D   **Use a FAP case conceptualization.** As discussed in Point 17, FAP case conceptualization essentially involves speculating about how your client's stated problems and goals for therapy may show up in the therapy room and then asking questions and observing your client to confirm or modify those hypotheses over time. The therapist may ask "out-to-in" parallel questions about possible in-session instantiations of out-of-session behavior, as in, "I understand how you have been reacting to your husband when he gets home late from work; do you think you would have that same reaction to me if I were late to start our session?" Asking such questions that parallel out-of-session and in-session behavior is a standard tool to help with the identification of possible CRBs.

Increased awareness in session requires a heightened sensitivity and connection to your client. In casual conversation, it is often enough to be paying partial attention to your partner, but in FAP the therapist is fully focused and completely in the moment with the client to an unusual degree. The therapist is completely attentive to the subtleties of the therapeutic interaction and is able to detect subtle shifts in client mood and behavior. The therapist is deeply connected to the client's history of hurts and successes, losses and gains. This exquisite sensitivity can be cultivated through therapist mindfulness practice and other efforts to be fully present, emotionally and interpersonally, to intimate partners.

It is important for the therapist to enter the session with a clear head and an open heart, fully devoted to the interpersonal experience that is about to occur with the client. Likewise, it is also important for therapists to develop this capacity for deep awareness and compassion in his or her own personal relationships—to be aware of his or her own T1s and T2s and work to improve these issues.

The FAP therapist will focus on the role of therapist in-session problem behaviors and therapist in-session target behaviors because an increased awareness of oneself goes hand-in-hand with an increased awareness of one's experience of clients. We recommend that therapists set aside time to explore questions such as:

- What do you tend to avoid addressing with your clients?
- How does this avoidance impact the work that you do with these clients?
- What do you tend to avoid dealing with in your life (e.g., tasks, people, memories, needs, feelings)?
- How do your daily life avoidances impact the work that you do with your clients?
- What are the specific T2s you want to develop with each client based on his/her case conceptualization?

Finally, the cultivation of increased awareness applies not only to clients' clinically relevant behaviors, but also to one's immediate and long-term impact on clients. It is essential that therapists assess the degree to which behaviors intended to reinforce actually functioned as reinforcers. The only way a therapist truly knows that a response intended to be reinforcing actually was reinforcing is by observing a long-term change in the frequency or intensity of the target behaviors.

20

Courage (Rule 2)

Implementing the steps to create an evocative therapeutic relationship often entails therapists taking risks and pushing their own intimacy boundaries. Such risks involve being courageous, venturing, persevering, and withstanding fear of difficulty. Doing FAP well often involves stretching one's limits and going outside of one's comfort zone.

Structuring therapy with the FAP rationale (the FAP rap)

From the very first contact, therapists can begin structuring the therapeutic environment to prepare the client for an intense and evocative therapy that focuses on in vivo interactions, by describing the FAP rationale ("FAP rap"). In order for FAP to be most effective, it is important that clients understand its premise—that the therapist will be looking for ways that clients' outside life problems show up within the therapy relationship because such an in vivo focus facilitates the most powerful change. This is an atypical idea regarding therapy as most people think they go into therapy to talk about problems and relationships outside of the therapy. Thus, variations of the FAP rap are presented in the initial phone contact, in the client informed consent form, and in the early sessions of treatment until the client understands it thoroughly.

Various examples of the FAP rap might include:

"I will be attempting to identify ways your daily life problems emerge within our therapy relationship, because such an in vivo focus facilitates the most powerful change."

"A primary principle in the type of therapy I do is that our relationship is a microcosm of your outside relationships. So I will be exploring how you interact with me in a way that is similar to how you interact with other people, what problems come up with me that also come up with other people, or what positive behaviors you have with me that you can translate into your relationships with other people."

"One focus of our therapy will be on how you can become a more powerful person, someone who can speak your truth compassionately and go after what you want. The most effective way for you to develop into a more expressive person is to start right here, right now, with me, to tell me what you are thinking, feeling needing, even if it feels scary or risky. If you can bring forth your best self with me, then you can transfer those behaviors to other people in your life."

"Our connection provides an opportunity for you to explore how you are in a relationship, for you to experiment with different ways of relating, and then to take it to your other relationships."

"Therapy has a greater impact when you talk about your experience in the present moment rather than reporting about things felt during the week. When we look at something that is happening right now, we can experience and understand it more fully and therapeutic change is stronger and more immediate."

A more detailed discussion of this topic, along with examples of how the form of the FAP rap can be tailored to match a range of therapist styles and comfort zones, is given in Point 16.

Focusing on FIAT-Q response classes

As discussed in Point 18, some therapists may find it helpful to administer the FIAT-Q (Callaghan, 2006a) to clients, and to go over with them possible CRB1s based on their FIAT-Q responses (see pp. 64–66 in Tsai et al., 2009c). Possible therapist behaviors that may be evocative of CRB1s in each of the response classes include:

Class A   (Assertion of needs): Asking certain kinds of questions. "What do you need from me, from this treatment?" "What would make this a really good session for you?" "How do you feel when I take your needs seriously?" "How did you feel when I said no to your request?"

Class B   (Bi-directional communication): Giving client appreciations and positive feedback, engaging in exercises where both therapist and client give each other positive feedback, asking for and giving constructive criticism, letting the client know his or her impact, asking for more eye contact, asking for body language to match verbal expression.

Class C   (Conflict): Bringing up topics that may potentially cause conflict.

Class D   (Disclosure and interpersonal closeness): Prompting more client self-disclosure, providing therapist self-disclosure if relevant to increasing closeness with client, letting the client know what s/he does that blocks closeness and inviting behaviors that increase closeness.

Class E   (Emotional experience and expression): Prompting more client emotional experience and expression, self-disclosing therapist emotional experience in response to client, helping client with emotion regulation or containment if overly emotional.

For more detail on ways to evoke CRBs, please refer to pp. 70–83 in Tsai et al. (2009c).

Using evocative therapeutic methods

FAP is an integrative therapy and calls for varied therapeutic techniques depending on what will evoke client issues and what will be naturally reinforcing of client target behaviors. What is important is not the theoretical origin of a specific technique but its function with a particular client. To the extent that a technique—any technique—functions to help clients contact and express avoided thoughts and feelings and other CRB1s, and evoke CRB2s that can be naturally reinforced, it is potentially useful to FAP (see Point 26).

Techniques often borrowed from other therapeutic approaches include: free association, timed writing exercises (e.g., writing whatever comes to mind without censoring), empty chair work, evoking emotion by focusing on bodily sensations, and evoking a client's best self using visualization. Such techniques are viewed functionally. That is emotional expressions (e.g., grief or a remembered trauma) are not described as a "release of energy" or "getting out of repressed feelings", but rather the expression is considered a CRB2, related to being more open, that will build and strengthen interpersonal closeness.

The general point is that almost any technique can be borrowed from other approaches if employed functionally and used to evoke CRBs. FAP therapists do not need to look like behavior therapists. They need to act like behavior therapists, which means being willing to try techniques that traditionally have not been labeled "behavioral" but doing so in a way that clarifies and uses their functions. In this way, the FAP therapist practices a technical eclecticism in the service of evoking CRBs that never loses its functional, behavioral foundation. Some behavior therapists may be reluctant to stray from specific techniques that they have been taught are the right "behavioral" techniques. We find this to be unnecessarily limiting. It greatly restricts the potential power of FAP. We encourage therapists to challenge themselves in this regard by exploring new techniques with a "try it and see" attitude, while always looking at the function, not the form, of techniques employed.

21

Therapeutic love (Rule 3)

Therapists' reinforcing behaviors that resemble and function similarly to genuine and caring relationships in the clients' community
are considered to be naturally reinforcing, and according to our
behavioral definition, can be described as "therapeutically loving."
Therapeutic love is ethical, is always in the clients' best interests,
and is genuine. Being therapeutically loving does not necessarily
mean using the word "love" with clients, but it does entail caring
deeply and fostering an exquisite sensitivity and concern for
improving your clients' daily lives, being governed by your clients'
best interests, and being reinforced by their improvements. It means
possessing your clients' goal repertoires, matching your expectations with your clients' current repertoires, and amplifying your
feelings to increase their salience to your clients.

Before discussing these qualities in more detail, we begin by first
attending to the best ways for therapists to respond to CRB1s. This
is an important issue because blocking CRB1s is closely tied to
evoking and reinforcing CRB2s.

Responding to CRB1s

Addressing CRB1s often involves making therapeutic use of negative personal reactions representative of the client's community,
such as, "It's hard for me to track what you are saying when you
don't make eye contact with me." It is important to underscore,
however, that CRB1s are addressed in the context of: (a) therapist
caring and concern for the client; (b) a conceptualization of the
client's problems in terms of historical and environmental factors
rather than as something "inside" or inherent in the client; (c) a
client's concurrence that certain behaviors are in-session problems

connected with daily life problems; and (d) the therapist's belief in the client's ability to produce more adaptive behavior in response to pointing out a CRB1 in the moment.

It is best to address CRB1s after the client has experienced a great deal of natural positive reinforcement from the therapist and a solid therapeutic relationship has formed, and after a client has given permission for the therapist to do so (e.g., "We've talked about how it's a problem for people to track you when you go off on tangents. Is it ok for me to interrupt you when you do that with me?"). If possible, it is best to address or block a CRB1 after the client already has emitted a CRB2 counterpart. For example, a therapist can say, "You know how sometimes you are really able to let yourself feel your sadness with me? What's stopping you from doing that right now?" Remember that your tone of voice and other non-verbal cues (leaning forward, moving your chair closer) also act as reinforcers. In general, we call for compassionate responses to CRB1s unless that has not worked in the past or the CRB1 calls for a more stern tone.

It is also important when responding to CRB1s to ensure that the session is not dominated by CRB1s and that the session does not end on a negative CRB1 note. The therapist, when responding to CRB1s, is in fact not so much trying to punish CRB1s as he or she is trying to evoke CRB2s, and if the therapist determines that it is unlikely that the client will successfully emit CRB2s in the session, it is probably a good idea to back away from FAP moves altogether rather than increasing the aversive qualities of the session by continuing to punish the client's behavior. Only in rare cases, for example when the client's behavior is life-threatening, should a therapist persist in punishing CRB1s in the absence of CRB2s. Clients in fact may be likely to drop out of therapy if sessions are dominated by responding to CRB1s rather than CRB2s.

Being governed by clients' best interests and reinforced by their improvements

Caring for clients means being governed by what is in their best interests and being reinforced by their improvements and successes.

The characteristics of a naturally reinforcing therapist are reminiscent of what Carl Rogers (1961) called for in his client-centered therapy: genuineness, empathy, and positive regard. Known for his opposition to "using reinforcement" to control others, Rogers would certainly not *try* to use it. Yet a careful analysis of his reactions to clients (Truax, 1966) indicates that Rogers reacted differentially to certain classes of client behavior. His caring and genuineness probably manifested as interest, concern, distress, and involvement that naturally punished CRB1s and reinforced CRB2s. Thus, we suggest that Rogers's call for genuineness and caring is an indirect method of enhancing the occurrence of naturally reinforcing contingencies.

Possessing clients' goal repertoires

Therapists are more able to discriminate client CRB1s and foster CRB2s when they have client goal behaviors in their own repertoires. For example, if a client is feeling invalidated by something her therapist said and shuts down, a therapist who is avoidant of conflict is unlikely to discriminate that the client is upset and is engaging in a CRB1 of pulling away and also unlikely to encourage an open discussion of what just happened between them. Thus, without the skills to address negative feelings, it is doubtful that the therapist will be able to resolve this conflict with the client and help the client do the same in her daily life relationships. Similarly, if a therapist is disdainful or afraid of client attachment and dependence (e.g., emailing the therapist several times a week, announcing feelings of dread and inability to cope at a therapist's upcoming vacation), the therapist will find it difficult to explore the client's feelings in a fruitful way. Helpful discourse may include exploring a client's history of unmet dependency needs and how this plays out in current relationships, and creating healthier ways of expressing attachment and dependency in both the therapeutic relationship and in daily life relationships.

Matching one's expectations with clients' current repertoires

Being aware of your clients' current repertoires will help you have reasonable expectations and tune into nuances of improvement.

Continuing with the example above of the client who felt extremely dependent on her therapist, it would not have been helpful to expect her to cheerfully wish her therapist "a great vacation," given that she felt suicidal upon thinking about her therapist going away. Instead, her behavior was shaped step by step over a period of 10 years, so that the therapeutic task, while difficult for her, matched what she was capable of in terms of her current repertoire: (1) going into the hospital while her therapist was on vacation; (2) meeting with a backup therapist while having telephone sessions with the primary therapist who was on vacation; (3) asking for a transition object (e.g., teddy bear) from the therapist and having sessions with a backup therapist without having phone sessions with the primary therapist; (4) asking for a little object from where the therapist was going to let her know the therapist was keeping her in mind; (5) not needing contact while her therapist was away by arranging to have lots of get-togethers with friends. While challenging, these therapeutic tasks did not feel impossible to her because they took place one by one over a period of 10 years. She has now reached a point in her therapy where she has a full social support network and sees her therapist once every 2 months.

Technically, we are talking here about the principle of shaping successive approximations to a desired target behavior, and CRB1s and CRB2s should be defined with shaping in mind. For example, although the ultimate goal for the above client was non-dependency on the therapist, if strict non-dependency were seen as the CRB2, the client never would have emitted any behavior that could have been reinforced by the therapist. The therapist's task is to identify graded improvements within the client's capability. What is an incremental improvement in terms of the client's current level of functioning? What would be a small, but real, stretch for this client?

The issue of shaping raises a certain complication for FAP. Specifically, although the therapist may be reinforcing CRB2s that are successive approximations to the target behavior, these CRB2s may not be reinforced by outside others. Thus, behaviors that are occurring in the therapy relationship will not generalize successfully to the outside world. For example, a very shy client's first attempt at assertiveness may be reinforced by the therapist, even though it was awkward and unlikely to meet with success in the outside world. Likewise, a client's first attempt at spending more time with his wife may be explained away by his wife as "you just want to get me off your back." This may be discussed directly with the client. The therapist may explain that the therapy relationship is an opportunity to practice and improve important interpersonal behaviors before "going on the road" with them. The therapist may also explain that as a therapist, s/he is probably more sensitive to subtle changes and more reinforced by them, because the therapist's only purpose in the relationship is to help the client. Real relationships are more complicated, and relationship partners may require time and patience before they change as well. The therapist, by being sensitive to the client's current level of functioning and being naturally reinforcing of even small improvements over current functioning, may foster in the client an appreciation for these small changes, such that they become self-reinforcing even in the absence of positive responses from others.

Amplifying one's feelings to increase their salience

Sometimes it is helpful for therapists to add explicit descriptions to their potentially reinforcing reactions in order to increase therapeutic effectiveness. Although the nature of the reinforcer is not fundamentally changed in this process, amplification can help clients discern therapists' private reactions that otherwise may be too subtle to be noticeable. To illustrate, consider a client who has difficulty in forming intimate relationships and who has taken a risk in revealing vulnerable feelings during the session. His disclosure results in subtle and spontaneous reactions in the therapist that include predispositions to act in caring ways and private respondents that correspond to "feeling close." Because these probably are not discriminated by the client (perhaps a CRB1 related to not being sensitive to subtle positive reactions in others) and thus would have weak reinforcing effects, the therapist describes private reactions by saying, "I feel really moved by what you just said." Without amplification, such important basic reactions would have little or no reinforcing effects on the client behavior that caused them. In saying this, the therapist may also be taking a risk and may be further evoking intimacy-related CRBs in the client.

22

Self-disclosure: using your personal reactions to clients

Therapist self-disclosure involves the sharing of information with a client that the client would not normally know or discover. It involves some risk and vulnerability on the part of the therapist and is a key element of FAP as it offers an authentic, natural, and often highly effective means of reinforcing or evoking CRBs and modeling effective behavior.

The notion of strategic use of therapist self-disclosure (Tsai, Plummer, Kanter, Newring, & Kohlenberg, 2010) stands in contrast to early psychotherapy traditions in which therapist anonymity was favored and therapist self-disclosure was considered a breach of the therapeutic frame (Edwards & Murdock, 1994). Since that time, however, theory and a growing body of research has advocated the judicious and strategic use of therapist self-disclosure in certain contexts (e.g., Barrett & Berman, 2001; Knox & Hill, 2003; Watkins, 1990). Interestingly, however, although theory and research support self-disclosure, the literature suggests that it is actually among the most infrequently used therapeutic strategies (Hill et al., 1988). This Point, therefore, will discuss the rationale behind therapist self-disclosure in FAP, offer some clinical examples of self-disclosure in action, and highlight therapist skills that increase the effectiveness of self-disclosure in session.

When the therapist has gained salience as a reinforcer, self-disclosures can be among the most powerful responses a therapist has to offer when they are strategically timed and genuine. When therapists express their personal reactions to CRBs, they provide essential data that clients may never have encountered previously about how their actions impact their relationships and the people around them. When a client's interpersonal behavior improves, the therapist's personal response to this improvement may be a rare and powerful gift given by the therapist to the client. For example, a client who has taken courageous steps in a session to reveal previously avoided material may feel particularly vulnerable at that moment. A therapist who feels a natural desire to disclose some vulnerability in response may hesitate for fear of crossing a therapeutic boundary. But a courageous and thoughtful disclosure by the FAP therapist at that moment may be quite powerful: for example, "Your courage right now gives me the courage to say to you that in this moment I feel vulnerable too. Right now, I feel we are in this together." This may have the effect of reinforcing the client's disclosure, enhancing the genuine intimacy of the therapeutic relationship, and establishing the therapeutic relationship as more similar to outside relationships, thus facilitating generalization. Another benefit of self-disclosure is that it gives clients explicit feedback on how the therapist feels and thus provides practice in learning how to read the subtle signs indicating how others feel.

Consider a client who originally presented with depression and anxiety symptoms and complained of feeling lonely despite her wide circle of friends, maintaining an illusion of herself as a perfectly happy professional, and feeling fraudulent. After six sessions during which the client generally maintained her veneer by being intellectual, humorous, and entertaining without being open and vulnerable (a CRB1), she cried as she disclosed for the first time her recent failed entrepreneurial venture and how it had led to a great deal of shame and fear of others' judgment. Recognizing this emotional opening as a significant CRB2, her therapist allowed herself to visibly tear-up as she listened, and subsequently explained how her client's CRB2s changed their relationship,

> "I have never understood so deeply the pain you've been carrying all by yourself for so long. And I am honored and moved that you trusted me and our relationship enough to show me your true self just now—it was honestly the most poignant moment I can remember in all of our sessions and makes me feel closer to you than I ever have before."

Such a disclosure by the therapist was likely to be naturally reinforcing for the client since it matches the reciprocity in healthy, intimate daily life interactions, where disclosures are often met with reciprocal disclosures.

While self-disclosure of a positive nature may be easier for most therapists, another important use of self-disclosure occurs when clients are behaving ineffectively. For example, consider a socially phobic client who avoids connection with others and wants to learn to build relationships. When he engages in CRB1s of mumbling and dropping off the ends of his sentences, a skilled FAP therapist might acknowledge in that moment what it feels like to be on the receiving end of the conversation,

> "I got some bits and pieces of what you were saying just then, but I noticed it was really hard for me to stay tuned in because of the mumbling and how your voice seemed to drop off inaudibly at the end. I felt as if one part of you wanted to connect, but another part was keeping me at arm's length so I couldn't engage with what you were saying."

This sort of self-disclosure explaining how the client's CRB1s detract from the therapist's ability to connect is compassionate while also likely punishing the client's CRB1s.

Therapist self-disclosures can happen on two different levels. The first level reveals the impact of client behaviors on the therapist's cognitive, affective, and physiological experience. This might include the therapist sharing a personal thought, memory, or emotion that was stirred by the client's CRBs. In the case of a physiological self-disclosure, the FAP therapist might use words to reveal any bodily reactions to the client's CRB (e.g., "I feel a warmth blossoming in my heart" or "My stomach is getting really tense all of a sudden") or may reveal these reactions more directly and non-verbally (e.g., sitting forward in the chair, tearing up, or emitting a deep belly laugh). These therapist behaviors may be more potent forms of self-disclosure at times as they go beyond the words of the intellect to expose the direct raw reaction of the therapist in a way that is less easily ignored or refuted by the client.

The second level of therapist self-disclosure occurs when the FAP therapist reveals something emotionally vulnerable about him- or herself. This covers a wide range including relevant life history, prevailing emotional circumstances that are impacting the session, previous struggles, or other information about the therapist's outside life. This type of therapist self-disclosure is typically used to reinforce the client or to model effective emotional expression, containment, or acceptance.

When using self-disclosure, it is important for therapists to remember a number of ideas.

1   First and foremost, self-disclosure is usually warranted when it is assessed to be in the client's best interest.
2   When self-disclosures are made, the therapist must assess their impact on the client (Rule 4), often requiring the therapist to ask directly, "How did you feel when you saw my tears?" or "How were you impacted hearing that I lost my father at a young age, too?". It is especially important not to assume that clients will be reinforced or shaped by specific therapist self-disclosures given that certain clinical populations have particular difficulty interpreting others' emotional expressions. Therapists must communicate with their clients in order to better gauge how self-disclosures should be formulated and delivered so as not to be lost in translation.
3   Therapists who use self-disclosure need to be aware of their own T1s and T2s so that they can discern which of their personal reactions are representative of the typical person with whom the client would interact, versus representing an idiosyncratic set of preferences or dislikes on the part of the therapist that may be the result of his/her reinforcement history. This is one of the main targets of FAP supervision (see Point 28)—to help therapists understand that perhaps their discomfort with some forms of emotional intimacy might misguide them to either extinguish or to give punishing self-disclosures to clients who

are exhibiting CRB2s. In short, "know thyself" before using self-disclosure in the therapy room.

4   When disclosing negative personal reactions to CRB1s, it is important to do so upon the foundation of a strong, well-established alliance. Once a case conceptualization has been created it is often effective to share with your client how their behaviors are influencing your emotions, thoughts, and physiology. For example, consider a client who has a strong tendency to get swept away in tangential storytelling in session, and complains that she often feels unheard in her relationships. Having established a strong alliance with this client, a therapist might say,

"I have to interrupt this story because I'm noticing that as you drift further and further into this story I'm drifting further and further away from the heart of your communication to me. I'm getting swept up into the details of the story, and I feel like I'm missing you. I know you've told me that you feel really unheard by the people in your life, like they don't understand you. And I'm wondering in this moment if there's something about this tendency to tell these grand stories that's contributing to this experience that you're having both with me and others in your life. Perhaps there's a different way for you to pinpoint the most important part of what you're trying to communicate to me through this story—if you could tell me directly."

In this way, the therapist disclosure exhibits/reveals understanding, concern, and compassion while also providing critical information about the immediate impact—in this case the ineffective immediate impact of the clients' habit of storytelling.

23

Homework (Rule 5)

Like all behavior therapies, FAP employs homework. In essence, homework is an assignment given to the client in the service of collecting data or information that can be used in structuring treatment and in practicing skills that help generalize therapeutic gains to daily lives. Homework assignments are used in FAP in three ways.

The first type of FAP homework is the generic kind found in almost all Cognitive Behavior Therapy (CBT) approaches. It entails asking the client to collect data and engage in activities specific to the CBT protocol being used. Examples include a daily CBT thought record (including challenges to assumptions) as discussed in Point 26, a Behavioral Activation activity log along with activation targets to be accomplished at planned times, or a record of the willingness to experience anxiety in evocative situations in an Acceptance and Commitment Therapy approach to anxiety disorders.

How we approach this type of FAP homework differs from standard CBT methods, however. While we believe in general that homework compliance improves outcome (Addis & Jacobson, 2000), and clients are encouraged to complete assignments, there is one important caveat. Employing FAP Rule 1, it is possible that homework compliance is a CRB1. For example, if a client's daily life problem involves uncritical compliance with what is asked of him or her, resulting in becoming over-committed and overwhelmed, homework completion may be a CRB1 of over-compliance. From a FAP perspective, this CRB1 of problematic compliance provides an opportunity for the therapist to see the client's problem in action and to set the scene for shaping and reinforcing more productive behavior (CRB2s) such as being more direct about anticipated problems or asking for either a delay or a decrease in the scope of the assignment in order to avoid over-commitment.

Conversely, noncompliance could be a CRB1, and its occurrence in the therapy provides an opportunity to do here-and-now trouble-shooting or perhaps deal with issues such as counter-control (known as "passive-aggressiveness" in non-behavioral terms) resulting from an oppressive over-controlling parent, fear of failure (e.g., "if I can't do it right, I will be a failure"), problems with distractibility (adult ADHD—attention deficit hyperactivity disorder), or organizational skills.

Homework assignments used by FAP therapists may emphasize interpersonal risks such as being vulnerable with others, being assertive, and expressing positive and negative feelings. Although assignments with an interpersonal focus are also used in standard CBT protocols, these are done to a greater extent by FAP-informed therapists. Further, some homework assignments are specific to FAP. For example, FAP therapists routinely assign the "session bridging" sheet after each session (see Appendix, Tsai et al., 2009c) to be turned in at the beginning of the next session. This form asks for feedback, both positive and negative, about various aspects of the session as well as inquiring about the degree of connection to the therapist. The session bridging sheet also asks "What issues came up for you in the session/with your therapist that are similar to your daily life problems?" Thus, the bridging sheet assignment helps to maintain a focus on the therapist–client relationship and on increasing awareness of CRB.

The second type of homework used in FAP entails requesting the client to practice in daily life a relationship skill that was developed within the context of the therapist–client relationship. This process can be facilitated by using Rule 5 interpretations. For example, consider a client who has difficulty in forming close relationships and has minimal or no eye contact with the therapist when s/he is struggling with expressing feelings. After this has been identified as a CRB1, and the CRB2 of increasing eye contact is an explicit within-session target that is reinforced in the here-and-now, the client might be asked to try to increase eye contact with others. Following Rule 5, it might be stated in the following way:

"When we first started our therapy, you tended to avoid feelings and reduce our connection by diverting your eyes. That created distance between us. After you became aware of this issue and were more willing to have eye contact with me and to express feelings, our relationship became closer. I'm going to suggest that you try to do the same thing with Carol (a friend) and see what happens to the closeness in your relationship with her."

The therapist then may schedule a very specific homework assignment for the client to do this with Carol.

The third type of homework may better be called "session work" which entails assigning clients to practice or apply what they have learned within the therapist–client relationship. Rather than requesting this practice be done with others in their real life, however, clients instead are requested to practice in session with the therapist, functionally also having features of "real life". We are not referring to "role-playing" but instead to actual, here-and-now, real-life behavior that occurs in the therapist–client relationship. Consider the following example. A client was exhausted after interacting with others and because of this suffered from stress-related physical symptoms. Her stress also resulted in her limiting her relationships to short exposures such as a "date", and excluded longer term relationships where a great deal of time was spent together. A major source of her stress was that she took full responsibility to make sure there were things to talk about, to be vivacious, animated, and interesting—in her words, she had to be "on." She perceived that her taking on this responsibility worked in that she was popular and pursued by men. Also, from her standpoint, it was necessary to assume this responsibility and put effort into "being on" because down deep she was not interesting or attractive and would not be sought after if she acted naturally and in a relaxed manner. As you might guess, she exhibited the same CRB1s during therapy. In each session, she hit the ground running, and was definitely interesting and vivacious. She would take a considerable amount of time before sessions planning how she would be interesting to the therapist. When this CRB1 was identified, the therapist assigned "session work." It was suggested that she try beginning sessions without a plan, sit back, take it easy, and instead more frequently leave it up to the therapist to come up with topics to talk about. In short, she was asked to give up her total responsibility for keeping the session interesting and instead share this responsibility with the therapist. Her initial reaction was that she did not know if she could do it, but she would try. Over the next few sessions she did try and these CRB2s were shaped and nurtured. Eventually, she was able to sit back, be relaxed, and more often wait for the therapist to bring up topics. She found the sessions less stressful and discovered that she naturally was interesting and able to engage the therapist in meaningful discussion. Eventually, the treatment involved the second type of homework assignment and she was requested to try these same behaviors with others in her daily life.

The three types of FAP homework assignments are all in the service of generalizing gains from treatment to daily life and can be used either singly or in combination.

24

Talking with clients (Rule 5)

A great deal of talking occurs during therapy sessions, and this rule identifies certain types of therapist talk of particular importance in FAP. A client might ask the therapist "Why did I do that?" or "Why am I so afraid of intimacy?" and the therapist is expected to give an answer. From a behavioral standpoint, the answer is just a bit of verbal behavior referred to as a "reason." FAP "reasons" are designed to help clients find solutions to their problems and to help generalize progress in therapy to daily life. A functionally analytically informed reason includes a history that accounts for how it was adaptive for clients to act in the ways they do. For example, being intimate and open not only is beneficial in forming and maintaining close relationships, but it also makes one vulnerable to punishment. For a particular client, his or her history might include a childhood and later period in which attempts at intimacy were punished. Clients who account for their lack of intimacy by referring to this history are better positioned to take risks in the future as a means to remedy the problem.

Parallels between in-session and daily life behaviors

Out-to-in parallels take place when daily life events are related to corresponding in-session situations, and *in-to-out parallels* occur when in-session events are related to corresponding daily life events. These parallels may facilitate the generalization of gains (Rule 5) made in the client–therapist relationship to daily life as well as assist in identifying CRB (Rule 1). Both types of parallels are important, and a good FAP session may involve considerable weaving between daily life and in-session content through multiple in-to-out and out-to-in parallels.

Facilitating generalization is essential in FAP. Below is an example based on an interaction between a FAP therapist and her client "Alicia" who participated in a 20-session treatment for depression and smoking cessation. They are talking about an out-to-in parallel that Alicia is struggling with regarding her pulling away once she knows someone cares about her.

Therapist: You know how I've said to you a number of times in our work together that our relationship is very, very important, and that it's a microcosm of your outside life relationships. [Rule 2: Evoke CRB. The therapist has been hypothesizing that Alicia cancelling her recent sessions due to back pain may be a CRB1 involving avoidance of the closeness that has been increasing in their therapeutic relationship (Rule 1: Be Aware of CRB).]

Client: Yeah I was thinking about that, and I kind of wrote about it on my session bridging sheet. When I think back to the relationships I've been in, all my boyfriends, I really relish the pursuit, but once they turn around and start liking me, I go "Yuk". Then I feel smothered. I realized I did that in this relationship too in a way.

Therapist: With me?

Client: Yeah it was like the excitement in the beginning, everything's new, then you really focused on me and turned your attention on me, and I froze. And I don't know why at a point when people reciprocate the energy I'm putting into it, then I freak out.

Therapist: Close relationships involving intimacy can bring about a lot of hurt, which you've certainly experienced in your relationships with men. So it makes sense that you might want to be cautious and pull away. That gives you more of a sense of control over the relationship, but it can also bring about the very outcome that you are trying to avoid [a Rule 5 interpretation]. It's so important that you can say this out loud, it's incredible, because I certainly felt you freaking out [Rule 3, natural reinforcement of what she is saying].

Client: . . . When relationships get to the stage where they matter to me, I have some kind of psychic time gauge, I have to reject it before I get rejected. If I sit it out and I'm convinced I won't be rejected right off the bat, I'm able to recommit myself.

Therapist: This is really important. I can't wait for you to get into a relationship, have this issue come up, and talk about it. I can't emphasize enough how connecting it is to have someone tell you what's going on, to have you tell me, this whole conversation we are having is just awesome. [Rule 3, more natural reinforcement; Rule 5, encouraging an in-to-out parallel.]

Providing functional analytically informed interpretations can help clients in two ways. First, the interpretation or reason can lead to a prescription, instruction, or rule. The interpretation, "You are acting toward your wife like you did toward your mother" can easily be taken as a prescription "Treat your wife more fairly since she obviously is not your mother, and your relationship will improve." Second, a reason can enhance the salience of controlling variables and increase reinforcement density by acting as a "signal." For example, a female client learns that the reason she feels rejected at times during the session is a function of the therapist's attentiveness level, and that this attentiveness is related to how late in the day it is. As a result, the client is in better contact (she notices that the therapist is less attentive when she sees him late in the day), and then experiences less aversiveness when he is inattentive.

The verbal repertoire to be developed by therapists involves statements that relate events during the session to the relationship symbolized by $S^d \cdot R \rightarrow S^r$. This represents operant behavior in which (1) S^d is the discriminative stimulus or prior situation whose influence over the occurrence of R varies with the reinforcement history; (2) R is the response or operant behavior which is influenced by the S^d, and (3) S^r is the reinforcement or effect of the response on the environment. For example, "When I asked you how you are feeling about our therapeutic relationship (S^d), you responded by talking about your therapy goals (R), which is another topic that you know I'm interested in. I rewarded your avoidance by talking about therapy goals (S^r)."

As a general strategy, it is useful to interpret client statements in terms of functional relationships, learning history, and behavior. Downplaying mentalistic and non-behavioral entities, such as inadequate motivation, low self-esteem, lack of ego strength, fear of success, and instead emphasizing behavioral interpretations and history are useful to clients because attention is directed to external factors that lend themselves to therapeutic interventions.

25

A logical therapeutic interaction in FAP

FAP's five rules may be applied flexibly and functionally, thus application of FAP may look quite different from one client to another, because each client's CRBs and what is reinforcing of those CRBs may be quite different. In our experience, however, we have found that some powerful FAP interactions follow a logical in-session sequence. Here we describe some commonalities that appear across the authors' experiences of these powerful in-session FAP sequences. An important aspect of this 12-step sequence is that FAP's five rules are instantiated in order from Rule 1 to Rule 5 as the interaction proceeds. Thus the interaction is a demonstration of FAP in total. Specifying the interaction at the level of the moment-to-moment therapist–client interaction may be helpful for both training and research purposes.

The interaction assumes that a good strong FAP relationship is already in place. The therapist: (a) is deeply in touch with the contingencies of reinforcement that have shaped his or her client; (b) is feeling deep compassion for the client's history of wounds and losses; and (c) is aware of the client's CRB1s and CRB2s in the context of this history (Rule 1). In session, the therapist also is maintaining strong connection with the client using eye contact and body language that conveys compassion. Finally, in addition to contingently reinforcing improvements, the therapist is providing a solid explicit foundation of validation of what the client is disclosing both in the moment and over the course of therapy.

In this context, here now is the logical interaction. It starts with the client and therapist having a discussion about daily life material.

1 **Therapist out-to-in parallel**. The therapist provides an out-to-in parallel (Rule 1), drawing a parallel between events in the

client's daily life and what is happening in the therapy relationship: "The way you are talking about protecting yourself with your husband, do you feel that you have to protect yourself with me, too?"

2   **Client confirmation of accuracy of the parallel**. The client confirms the accuracy of the parallel: "Yes." Of course, sometimes parallels will not be accurate, and that is fine. Not everything in the client's life needs to have an in-session parallel in FAP.

3   **Therapist evokes CRB**. With the parallel confirmed, the therapist evokes CRB (Rule 2) with respect to the behavior: "How about right now, could you drop your guard and be a little more real with me? I'd really like to see it."

4   **Client emits CRB1**. Typically, the first time CRB is evoked, it will be CRB1 of avoidance: "I don't know, that would be really hard." Of course, ideally there will be few CRB1s and CRB2s instead will be evoked. Although the therapist is never hoping for CRB1, s/he is prepared for them.

5   **Therapist contingently responds to CRB1**. In response, the therapist contingently responds to the CRB1 (Rule 3), by blocking the avoidance and re-presenting the evocative question: "I understand how hard it is for you. Still I think you are strong, and I believe you can let your guard down a bit right now. How about if you take a breath and try?"

Loops in which steps 4 and 5 are repeated several times are common in the logical FAP interaction. The client avoids, the therapist blocks it and tries again to evoke CRB2; the client continues to avoid, and the therapist continues compassionately to gently block and evoke. Essentially, an "extinction struggle" is occurring: Will the client's CRB1 avoidance behavior extinguish or will the therapist's attempts to block CRB1 and evoke CRB2 extinguish? The therapist should be gauging the client's tolerance for this extended struggle, because it is important in FAP for the session to stay positive and constructive, to focus on CRB2s, not CRB1s, and thus to view even very small improvements in the client's behavior as CRB2s.

6 **Client emits CRB2**. The client engages in CRB2: "Well, I appreciate you saying that. I do want to be more genuine in here; it is just so hard for me to be real (crying)." When CRB2 such as this takes place, the fundamental moment in FAP has occurred.

7 **Therapist contingently responds to CRB2**. The therapist contingently responds to the CRB2 with natural reinforcement (Rule 3):

"Well, I really feel you right now, my heart is completely open to you, and I am filled with compassion for what you are going through. When you cry like this, I have this exquisite sense of your pain and all you have gone through. While I know you don't like to cry in front of people, right now you doing so makes me feel closer to you, and I will not hurt you."

Much of FAP training is about helping FAP therapists respond well to CRB2s—genuinely, compassionately, fully, and immediately. Each FAP therapist will have his or her own style in doing so, and the response above should not be emulated as the "correct" response. We do believe, however, it is important to notice that the response above is full and long. We want the reinforcing response to be extremely salient, clear, and unambiguous to the client. We want the client to have no doubt how the therapist feels in response to the CRB2.

8 **Client engages in more CRB2**. The client emits more CRB2: "When you say that, it is really hard to hear, but somehow I believe you (crying more)." When clients respond to the therapist's attempt to do Rule 3 with more CRB2, that is confirmation that Rule 3 was effective (Rule 4). The best interactions in FAP are when loops occur in which steps 7 and 8 repeat: the therapist reinforces CRB2, the client engages in more CRB2, the therapist reinforces the new CRB2, and the client continues to engage in more CRB2. In this way, CRB2s quickly and powerfully can be shaped and strengthened. Oftentimes, these interactions are

characterized by both client and therapist vulnerability, in which both are feeling the discomfort that comes with true rapid increases in intimacy.

9 **Therapist engages in Rule 4**. The therapist asks about the effect of his or her response to the client (Rule 4): "So how was all that for you?" The therapist should not rush into this step; in fact it could happen during the next session. The primary issue is that the Step 7–8 loop in which CRB2s are shaped should come to a natural end and not be rushed. Once the interaction has naturally stopped, the remaining steps in the interaction are about "processing" and generalizing the interaction.

10 **Client indicates that the interaction was reinforcing**. The client suggests that the therapist was reinforcing: "I feel relieved, good." This processing of the interaction is helpful in assessing what is reinforcing to the client, but the therapist should keep in mind that in FAP, reinforcement is defined functionally as that which increases client behavior, not by what the client reports s/he liked. Therefore, Rule 4 primarily is about observing the impact of the therapist's response on the client's behavior over time. Nonetheless, immediate feedback on the impact of the interaction as per this step is often useful to the therapist.

11 **Therapist engages in Rule 5**. The therapist provides a functional description of the interaction, an in-to-out parallel and homework assignment based on the interaction (Rule 5):

"Well, it seems to me that what just happened is that you took a risk and let your guard down. I responded by letting you know how I felt when I saw you do that, which in turn helped you open up even more, and now you feel relieved and good [functional interpretation]. I am wondering what would happen if you were like this more often with your spouse [in-to-out parallel]? Do you think we can spend a few minutes now talking about what you can do differently with your spouse [leading to homework assignment]?"

12 **Client expresses willingness to engage in homework**. The

final step in the interaction is the client expressing willingness to try the new behavior in his or her daily life.

Overall, this logical interaction consists of three phases. First, with steps 1, 2, and 3, the issue is awareness of CRBs and bringing CRBs into the room. Then, with steps 4 through 8, the issue is shaping of CRB2s—this is the heart of FAP. Finally, the third phase consists of processing and generalizing the interaction. When all 12 steps occur, we expect FAP interactions to be more powerful and lasting than when the interaction is only partially completed. Exploring this hypothesis is an important research direction for FAP.

26

Openness to techniques from other therapies

With rare exceptions, every therapist reading this book has learned a variety of therapeutic approaches other than FAP. Further, many of you have an allegiance, preference, and skill set for at least one type of therapy. The main question addressed in this chapter is "How can FAP enhance the work of therapists whose ongoing practice is based on other approaches?" From its inception FAP was presented as an integrative therapy (Kohlenberg & Tsai, 1994) that can be used as either a stand-alone treatment or as an add-on intended to enhance other approaches (Kohlenberg & Tsai, 1991). Here we will focus on the add-on feature.

Two principles are involved in using FAP to enhance or add on to other approaches. First, the techniques, methods, forms, guidelines, and goals of the approach to be enhanced continue to be used (with minimal modifications) along with the FAP add-ons. The idea is that adding FAP (as illustrated below for cognitive therapy) builds and capitalizes on the existing skills of the therapist as well as on methods developed in the alternative approach. In this way, the FAP enhancement is intended to be user friendly in that it is integrated into the therapist's existing therapeutic repertoire and does not require learning a new treatment.

The second principle is the underlying FAP notion that contingencies of reinforcement for client improvements—occurring in the here-and-now during the session in the relationship between the client and therapist—are a potentially powerful mechanism for producing significant psychotherapeutic change. In other words, it is important to use here-and-now interventions as much as possible. Accordingly, FAP interventions center on the therapist recognizing (being aware of) the real-life improvements that occur in relationship to the therapist, and in turn, nurturing, shaping, and naturally reinforcing these improvements at the moment they occur—in FAP parlance, noticing CRB (Rule 1) and reinforcing CRB2 (Rule 3).

To some readers, the first and second principles may appear incompatible. This likely is due to a misunderstanding as to what we mean by "client improvements." Improvements, however, are idiographically defined, and thus can embrace the goals of other therapies depending on the context, history, and objectives of each client. Examples include: intimate relating, being vulnerable in close relationships, replacing distorted thinking (cognitive distortions) with more accurate and balanced thinking, testing cognitive hypotheses, altering attachment styles, getting in touch with and expressing hidden feelings, remembering early trauma, being mindful, explaining one's own problems by describing the relationship between early childhood experience and present behavior, and acting in accordance with values rather than emotions.

The following example illustrates how the two principles were used to integrate Cognitive Therapy with FAP. Cognitive Therapy, also known as Cognitive Behavior Therapy (CBT), is a treatment that enjoys extensive empirical support for a wide range of disorders. In the service of illustrating a FAP enhancement, we will focus on just one aspect of the rich and rather complex approach originally proposed by Beck and colleagues (Beck et al., 1979).

The cognitive hypothesis states that an antecedent event evokes dysfunctional cognition that in turn causes problematic emotional and behavioral responses. Treatment involves identifying these dysfunctional cognitions and attempting to replace them with more reasonable and accurate cognitions. A standard CBT therapeutic tool used to accomplish this goal is the assignment to clients of a daily "thought record," a type of diary that includes columns labeled "life situations," "cognitions or beliefs," and the occurrence of "problematic emotional responding and/or behavior." The thought record is then discussed during the therapy session, and alternative more reasonable and accurate cognitions are then explored.

Another CBT method is to urge the client to test the accuracy of the dysfunctional assumption by engaging in the avoided behavior between therapy sessions to see if the dysfunctional assumption is supported by reality. For example, consider a depressed client whose daily thought record indicates he does not express dissatisfaction or make requests for what he needs because he assumes terrible things will happen. Using the first FAP principle, a suggested FAP enhancement is to use the CBT daily record with the relatively minor addition of another column that asks "Does this happen during the therapy session in relationship to the therapist?" This addition will help the therapist to notice (Rule 1) whether the problematic emotion or dysfunctional belief (a CRB1) is happening in the here-and-now consistent with the second FAP principle. Similarly, if the dysfunctional belief is occurring during the therapeutic session, the client can be asked to test the accuracy of the assumption (consistent with the first principle) by expressing wants and or dissatisfactions to the therapist (the second principle) to test whether "terrible things will happen." The result is that an opportunity is now available for significant improvement due to the power of immediate reinforcement for therapeutic change as it actually is occurring (as opposed to exclusively talking about making these changes in the upcoming week). Thus, rather than just talking about dysfunctional beliefs and ways to alter them, the FAP enhancement enables them to be actually practiced in vivo. A particularly powerful advantage of focusing on the therapist client interaction during CBT is that dysfunctional beliefs concerning interpersonal relationships can be identified, challenged, and modified in the here and now.

Data suggest that FAP techniques can be learned and integrated into practice by experienced cognitive therapists without compromising the adherence and competence (quality) of the CBT as determined by independent experts (Kohlenberg et al., 2002). Adding FAP techniques into CBT produces improvements in client interpersonal functioning and improves the durability of the treatment. In fact, the most powerful sessions of these therapists were those that involved in-the-moment identification and modification of dysfunctional beliefs (Kohlenberg et al., 2002).

The integration of FAP with modalities other than CBT has been discussed in connection with couples therapy (Gurman, Waltz, & Follette, 2010), psychodynamic therapy (Rosenfarb, 2010), mindfulness (Kohlenberg et al., 2009b), Mode Deactivation Therapy (Apsche, Ward, & Evile, 2002; Houston, Apsche, & Bass, 2007), and group therapy (Hoekstra & Tsai, 2010). Given its shared theoretical coherence, FAP is particularly amenable to integration with Acceptance and Commitment Therapy (ACT; Hayes et al., 1999), Behavioral Activation (BA; Martell et al., 2010; Lejuez, Hopko, Acierno, Daughters, & Pagoto, 2011), and Dialectical Behavior Therapy (DBT; Linehan, 1993). For more detailed discussions of these integrations see Kohlenberg and Callaghan (2010) and Luciano (1999) for ACT; Busch, Manos, Rusch, Bowe, and Kanter (2010b) and Manos et al. (2009) for BA; and Waltz, Landes, and Holman (2010) for DBT.

27

Termination

Termination of therapy is likely to be difficult for both the client and the therapist, especially if a strong relationship has been formed. Therefore, the subject of termination should be raised early, so that both participants can have a number of sessions to discuss the ending of therapy.

Since FAP is an idiographic treatment, however, just as there is no set length of time for treatment, there is no set number of sessions needed to process termination. Timing may vary depending on the length of treatment. In short-term or time-limited therapy, the client and therapist may know at the outset that treatment only will consist of 20 sessions or a given number of months. In long-term treatment, termination may be expected to occur once the client and therapist agree that goals have been met or that sufficient progress has been made.

Termination is an opportunity to help the client build a new repertoire for loss and endings. Often, relationships in the outside world do not end well. Sometimes they end cordially, sometimes angrily, and on some occasions people just gradually slip apart without ever saying goodbye. But rarely is the ending (except perhaps when a death is imminent and is being prepared for) seen as an opportunity to truly explore its meaning and to feel it fully. FAP therapists strive for such meaningful endings.

The therapist may initiate a conversation about termination by saying something such as, "Endings and loss are a part of life and relationships, and therapy and the therapeutic relationship allow for a unique opportunity to end an important relationship thoughtfully by acknowledging the impact we have had on each other." A question that can be explored in great detail is, "For many clients, the end of therapy brings up feelings and memories of previous transitions and losses. What thoughts and feelings do endings in general bring up for you? What thoughts and feelings are you having about the ending of this therapy relationship?" Given that the therapist will have a well-formed and evolved case conceptualization of the client, s/he should then determine if the client's responses are CRB1s or CRB2s and then respond appropriately.

FAP therapists also may choose to write an end-of-therapy letter—such a letter can be an important component of the parting process. The letter may include a description of progress made, what the therapist appreciates about the client, any interactions that were moving to the therapist or stood out during therapy, what the therapist will remember or take away from therapy, what the therapist wants the client to take away, hopes and wishes for the client, and parting advice. These are also types of issues the client and therapist should discuss when talking about termination. Providing clients with a closing letter gives them something tangible to take away from therapy and a concrete reminder of their progress and the therapeutic relationship.

The final phase of FAP is a time to consolidate gains and to ensure that the positive interactions that have taken place in the therapeutic relationship have generalized to the clients' outside lives. It is a chance to model how a relationship can end positively, with meaning and feeling. Clients should have a clear sense of the ways in which they are special and clarity about what they have to contribute to the relationships in their lives, their communities, and perhaps the world.

28

Supervision and training

As experiential as it is didactic, FAP supervision and training empha-size the self-development of the therapist and the establishment of ten core competencies in conducting FAP: (1) creating a behavior analytic case conceptualization; (2) understanding CRBs as functional classes, not topography; (3) identifying CRBs; (4) responding to CRB1s effectively; (5) evoking CRBs; (6) responding to CRB2s effectively; (7) expressing a naturally reinforcing repertoire of warmth, trust-establishment, risk-taking, and self-disclosure; (8) demonstrating awareness of reinforcement impact; (9) demonstrating awareness of T1s and T2s; and (10) providing functional analytically informed interpretations and implementing generalization strategies.

This point delineates a conceptual framework that facilitates an understanding of the FAP supervision and training process (Callaghan, 2006b; Kohlenberg & Tsai, 1991; Tsai, Callaghan, Kohlenberg, Follette, & Darrow, 2009a; Follette & Callaghan, 1995).

Consistent with supervision across all theoretical orientations, the first goal of FAP supervision and training is to increase the super-visee's knowledge base and critical and conceptual clinical thinking skills. This goal is accomplished via modeling of competence, specific instructions (including reading assignments), goal setting, and feedback on performance (Milne & James, 2000). The FAP knowledge base consists of a verbal repertoire for describing the important features of the therapeutic process: for example, (1) devel-oping a case conceptualization in order to understand which client behaviors may be CRB1s and CRB2s; (2) evoking and naturally reinforcing CRB2s; and (3) conducting a functional analysis of T1s and T2s that occur during treatment and supervision.

The second goal of FAP supervision and training is to directly shape and increase the effectiveness of therapist behavior related to noticing, evoking and strengthening CRBs. These therapist behaviors are contingency-shaped and, unlike improvements in the FAP knowledge base, improvements in contingency-shaped behavior can occur outside of awareness. This sort of knowledge is described in everyday language as "deep," "emotional," and "intuitive" (Skinner, 1974).

In FAP supervision, therapist behavior is learned through direct exposure to an intense interpersonal relationship with the supervisor, in which emitting and noticing important behaviors occur. Safran and Muran (2001) similarly suggest that in supervision, as in therapy, all interactions take place within a relational context. They contend that supervision should include in vivo experiential opportunities because learning primarily at a conceptual level is insufficient. The contrast between intellectual knowing versus emotional knowing through supervision is aptly described by one supervisee.

"Many other supervisors tried to teach me to be emotionally present with my clients. But I am finding that going there is something I do heart-first. To do this task, I needed more than hearing it in supervision, reading it in an article, or watching it on a video. I needed to experience it myself, in vivo, within the supervisory relationship. That, for me, is the core of FAP and FAP supervision that is transforming me and my work."

The supervision methods described below delineate a range of ways supervisors can create powerful relationships with their supervisees. Such relationships aim to create profound moments in which supervisees experience large personal gains that make them more effective FAP therapists.

Create a "sacred" space for supervision

Just as FAP therapists create a sacred therapeutic space for their clients, FAP supervisors create a similar sacred space for their supervisees. As stated in Point 15, a "sacred" space is exclusively dedicated to some person or special purpose, protected by sanction from incursion. Whether or not it is labeled in this way, the key is that

FAP supervisors create an environment in which supervisees can feel safe and deeply cared for as they learn how to implement FAP. Just as in therapy, this is achieved by establishing a genuine relationship, explicitly describing the rationale for supervision, and maximizing positive reinforcement during supervision. Functionally, the more sacred and positively reinforcing the supervisory space, the more likely the supervisee will take risks, leading to major repertoire changes that can be transforming.

Focus on in vivo work when appropriate

It is important in FAP supervision to focus on in vivo work that is relevant to the supervisee's growth as a therapist. This is done through contingent natural reinforcement of supervisee target behaviors in the context of the sacred space and the real relationship between the supervisor and the supervisee.

The supervisor may evoke and naturally reinforce key supervisee target behaviors that apply to FAP, such as being aware, being courageous, and being therapeutically loving. FAP supervisors and supervisees should together determine what the supervisees' T1s and T2s are, and the supervisor should be sensitive to these as they occur in the supervisory relationship. Because supervision is not therapy, supervisors may choose to disclose in more detail than they would with a client what their own 1s and 2s are with the supervisee, and may be open to the supervisee being explicitly reinforcing of the supervisor's improvements as well. Typical targets in supervision include decreasing avoidance and increasing courage. Decreased avoidance by therapists involves taking risks, having and expressing feelings (such as caring, sadness, anger), being vulnerable, asking someone in pain to do difficult things, facing one's own fear and asking others do the same, and welcoming silence, criticism, conflict, or disagreement.

By responding to supervisee T1s and T2s, the FAP supervisor also provides a model to the supervisee of the process of implementing FAP rules (being aware of CRBs, evoking CRBs, naturally reinforcing CRB2s, being aware of one's impact, and providing functional analytic interpretations). For example, being therapeutically loving is an important aspect of Rule 3, equated with being naturally reinforcing and with being reinforced by your supervisees' improvements and successes. Being therapeutically loving is a broad class of therapy behaviors that supervisors can model contextually, and such training is likely to be relevant to supervisees' therapeutic work. The supervisory relationship can become intimate and profound as supervisors demonstrate therapeutic love, and supervisees' experience of this process may facilitate their engagement in it with clients.

Thus, FAP supervisors are authentic in describing their thoughts and feelings to their supervisees, and they see, evoke, value, and reinforce their supervisees' best qualities, evoking descriptions such as, "You mirror back to me the best of who I am, and you see the best of who I am capable of becoming." Like FAP therapy, the intensity of FAP supervision will vary depending on the needs and repertoires of the supervisees, and supervisee progress will be shaped over time.

29

Ethical issues and precautions

FAP seeks to create a deep and profound therapeutic experience; the degree of thoughtfulness, care, and caution that FAP therapists bring to their work must be equally deep and profound. Ethical codes developed to guide therapists in general, such as the APA Ethical Guidelines (*Ethical Principles of Psychologists and Code of Conduct*, 2010 Amendments) are relevant and applicable to FAP. Specific characteristics of FAP ensure some of these guidelines are particularly salient. The following sections delineate areas of potential ethical concern and the ways they relate to FAP.

Avoid exploitation

Since the therapy relationship is one of unequal power, it is important to constantly keep in mind the question, "What is best for my client at the moment and in the long run?" Keeping this question at the forefront of treatment minimizes the likelihood of exploiting or harming clients through a host of situations that can be harmful to them: an unhealthy dependence on the therapist, sexual involvement, or interminable treatments where both parties are gratified by a relationship that is more like friendship than therapy.

The intensity and emotional intimacy that are often present in FAP relationships may increase the chances that sexual attraction will develop. FAP therapists must therefore have the best possible boundaries in this area. As described in the *Feminist Code of Ethics* (1999), therapists must not exploit clients sexually in an overt manner, but also should be aware of more subtle forms of sexual exploitation. For example, if a client has a CRB1 of seeking approval from others through sexualized behavior in a way that is detrimental to his or her sense of self, the FAP therapist must be able to identify this behavior and avoid reinforcing it.

Be aware of your cultural biases

Given that all of us have been shaped by the cultural contexts in which we have lived, FAP therapists must guard against defining client behaviors as CRB1s or CRB2s based solely on cultural expectations (Vandenberghe et al., 2010). When we are unaware of our biases, we may inadvertently reinforce a client for a behavior that is actually a CRB1 or punish a behavior that is a CRB2. For example, if the therapist expects men to be stoic, s/he may subtly punish emotional expression in a male client, even if such expression is a CRB2 for that person.

Acknowledging the importance of culture cannot be overstated. From a FAP perspective, after all, we are products of our environments, and culture is a primary factor in our environments. Thus, FAP therapists must be deeply attuned to a client's culture or subculture and get supervision when necessary to learn about a client's culture. What is reinforcing or punishing will vary depending on culture and FAP therapists must be skilled at assessing for cultural differences in the nature of CRBs and in what is naturally reinforcing of CRBs. FAP therapists also must be sensitive to the fact that language is a primary conveyor of culture and adapt their language accordingly. For example, in this book we have referred to the use of "therapeutic love." In the primary mainstream culture of the authors, the use of the phrase "therapeutic love" is meant to be slightly challenging and risky but never unethical or sexual. But in some cultures use of the word "love" in this context would signify a sexual relationship and would not be appropriate.

Understand your client thoroughly

FAP therapists take risks, evoke CRBs, and create intense therapeutic relationships. All of these experiences have the potential to be beneficial but also may be stressful and challenging, or even harmful for the client. The therapist therefore must proceed with caution and make careful use of principles of shaping. This requires knowing the client well, knowing what behaviors exhibited by the therapist will encourage growth and change at a level the client is ready for, and what behaviors will be overwhelming or off-putting in a way that leads to disengagement, undue distress, or even termination of therapy. FAP therapists are encouraged to carefully inform the client of the nature of the treatment (see Point 16 on the FAP rationale) but also to titrate the move into in-session focus in a way that the client can tolerate.

Be controlled by reinforcers that benefit clients

From a FAP perspective, a therapist who is controlled by reinforcers that are not beneficial to the client is a primary source of ethical violations. For example, the therapist may be reinforced by frequent expressions of gratitude and praise from a client for whom such behavior is a CRB1. If the therapist is unaware of this process, s/he may respond in a manner that reinforces and helps maintain the client's problem. Thus, it is exceedingly important that therapists recognize areas where they may be vulnerable to reinforcers that are not helpful to the client. In such instances, therapist supervision or consultation is thus always encouraged in FAP.

Increase your self-awareness

FAP encourages therapists to take risks; such risks must be taken in a context of clarity and self-awareness. Effective FAP therapists must have a high level of self-awareness, openness to examining their own motives and reinforcers, and an ability to recognize and respond to their own T1s non-defensively. Although this kind of self-awareness is important for all therapists, we believe it is particularly important in FAP because the therapist is being encouraged to take risks and evoke CRBs. For example, a therapist who is lonely or lacking intimacy in personal relationships may overly rely on therapeutic relationships for a primary source of closeness and be attracted to FAP as a means of increasing or justifying that intimacy. Such a therapist may place demands on the client for greater than appropriate closeness, under the guise of following FAP rules. It is crucial that FAP therapists examine their own responses and T1s in an ongoing way. Again, consultation and supervision are often a crucial part of such exploration.

Have the client's target behavior in your own repertoire

Many clients have difficulty accepting care and help, and have trouble being vulnerable, open, close, or intimate with others. With such clients, the FAP therapist needs to create a context in which there are opportunities to engage with the therapist in new, more connected ways. A therapist who is uncomfortable with closeness and is not addressing that limitation, is not likely to engage in behaviors that evoke connection or intimacy sufficiently with his or her client. The client may not be given the opportunity to work on essential issues around closeness in relationships or be reinforced for CRB2s in this area. Similarly, a therapist who is uncomfortable with intimacy, closeness, or vulnerability may be inclined to interpret a client's request for more connection, personal questions about the therapist, or expressions of reliance on the therapist as CRB1s in a broader class of dependence or neediness in relationships. For some clients, this may be the case, but it is clearly problematic if the therapist's own T1s are leading him or her to mistakenly assume the client's behavior reflects a CRB1 when it does not.

Alternatively, clients who have difficulty tolerating separation, solitude, or acting independently may need the therapist to help evoke and shape those behaviors. Again, a therapist who has difficulty with distance, autonomy or separation in relationships may inadvertently reinforce the client's CRB1s. S/he may not recognize these behaviors as CRB1s or create opportunities for CRB2s to occur.

These relationship capabilities involving both closeness and independence are examples of a wide range of behaviors that the FAP therapist ideally would strengthen in order to help clients develop similar behaviors. Just as a therapist who is phobic of heights is hindered in conducting an in vivo treatment for height-phobic clients, FAP therapists are more likely to be effective if they can engage in the behaviors they are helping their clients develop. FAP therapists must carefully evaluate the types of client problems they can effectively help by taking into consideration their own histories, behavioral repertoires, and current life limitations. They are strongly encouraged to address areas of limitation in their own psychotherapy and/or in supervision and consultation.

Do not continue a non-beneficial treatment

FAP-informed treatment does not help all clients. Research also clearly supports the importance of therapist–client match. Having therapy not work well is often emotionally evocative for therapists, and can result in problematic behavior such as blaming the client, directly or indirectly distancing from or being rejecting toward the client, becoming overly apologetic, self-critical, or tenaciously continuing therapy without acknowledging the lack of progress. At times, having a client decide not to continue treatment may represent an important CRB2, and FAP therapists must be able to reinforce this behavior.

30

The promise of FAP

FAP is about the transformative power of therapeutic love and inter-personal connection. FAP therapists strive to co-create intense and unforgettable relationships, to reflect what is special and precious about our clients by engaging in awareness, courage, love, and behaviorism—the essence of the FAP rules. As we model taking risks and speaking our truths compassionately, we challenge our clients to be more vulnerable and authentic and to bring forth their best selves.

This emphasis on the power of client vulnerability and authenticity is corroborated by the research of Brene Brown, a qualitative researcher who studies human connection and our ability to empathize, belong, and love. In a TED (Technology, Entertainment, Design) talk on "The power of vulnerability" (Brown, 2010), she shares a deep insight from her research—one that changed the way she lives, loves, and works.

Brown took the thousands of people she interviewed and divided them into those who have a sense of connection, worthiness, love, and belonging, and those who struggle for it. One variable separated them—people who felt connection had in common the courage to tell the full story of who they were. They lived with vulnerability, and they allowed themselves to be deeply and vulnerably seen. As a result of that authenticity, they had connection. The other thing they had in common was that they fully embraced vulnerability as necessary even though it was uncomfortable. They had a willingness to say "I love you" first, the willingness to do something where there were no guarantees, the willingness to invest in a relationship that might or might not work out.

Thus, the main finding of her research is that vulnerability is at the core of our struggle for connection, worthiness, joy, creativity, belonging, love. She states that

In order for connection to happen, we have to allow ourselves to be seen, to be vulnerable. . . . Our lives are a collection of stories and truths about who we are, what we believe, where we came from, how we struggle and how we are strong. When we can let go of what people think, and own our story, we gain access to our worthiness—the feeling that we are ENOUGH just as we are, and that we are worthy of LOVE and BELONGING.

(Brown, n.d.)

Not only does FAP increase clients' ability to connect and to give and receive love, but some FAP therapists are now incorporating a socially conscious ideology that also places a high importance on ecological, environmental, social justice, and non-violence goals, and using one's talents and passions to contribute to the world. Over recent years as global problems have intensified, we have proposed a variant of FAP that we term "Green" FAP, thus named because it encourages the overt introduction into therapy of personal therapist values that are consistent with the ideals of the "Green" movement (*Green Politics*, n.d.). Green FAP voices a concern for larger cultural issues and a plea to be in touch with what is possible. Green FAP urges us to: (1) claim a world where every life is precious; (2) love in a way we have never loved before; and (3) take our sense of personal agency to its highest level, applying our passions and gifts to personal, interpersonal, and global transformation (Tsai, Kohlenberg, Bolling, & Terry, 2009b).

While these aspirations guide our mission, FAP unquestionably requires that as scientists we closely follow the data, with a willingness to change direction if the data clearly tell us to do so. And while research on FAP is still in its infancy, the existing data are, in fact, supportive (Baruch et al., 2009b).

Micro-process analyses of moment-to-moment interactions, for example, in successful and unsuccessful FAP cases are starting to shed light on the precise mechanisms at work in FAP and how to maximize the impact of those interactions (Busch, Callaghan, Kanter, Baruch, & Weeks, 2010a; Busch et al., 2009). The emerging research is suggesting that in successful FAP cases, it may be very important to end FAP sessions with the reinforcement of CRB2, while unsuccessful FAP cases end with CRB1 (Kanter, 2010). These data also suggest that if FAP sessions are dominated by CRB1, in that FAP therapists are not able to successfully evoke CRB2, risk of drop-out is high. Thus, FAP therapists have a data-based reason to ensure that sessions are positive and focused on shaping improved behavior rather than punishing problem behavior.

Such research that directly informs clinicians speaks to the promise of FAP from a scientific perspective. Because FAP is based on a behavior analytic scientific framework that focuses both clinicians and researchers on the moment-to-moment interaction between the client and therapist, research on FAP's mechanism is directly relevant to clinical practice. Thus, the clinician may focus on creating a deep, meaningful, transformative relationship—the kind of relationship that truly matters to the client—and work with the confidence that what he or she is doing is in fact fully guided by science and supported by research. As such, FAP represents the epitome of the scientist-practitioner model. We hope this promise is further explored and nurtured by the next generation of clinicians and researchers.

References

Addis, M. E., & Jacobson, N. S. (2000). A closer look at the treatment rationale and homework compliance in cognitive-behavioral therapy for
depression. *Cognitive Therapy and Research*, *24*(3), 313–326.

American Psychiatric Association (2000). *Diagnostic and statistical manual
of mental disorders: DSM-IV-TR*. Washington, DC: American Psychiatric
Association.

Apsche, J. A., Ward, S. R., & Evile, M. M. (2002). Mode deactivation: A
functionally based treatment, theoretical constructs. *Behavior Analyst
Today*, *3*(4).

Barrett, M. D., & Berman, J. S. (2001). Is psychotherapy more effective
when therapists disclose information about themselves? *Journal of
Consulting and Clinical Psychology*, *69*, 597–603.

Baruch, D. E., Kanter, J. W., Busch, A. B., & Juskiewicz, K. (2009a).
Enhancing the therapy relationship in acceptance and commitment
therapy for psychotic symptoms. *Clinical Case Studies*, *8*, 241–257.

Baruch, D. E., Kanter, J. W., Busch, A. M., Plummer, M. D., Tsai, M.,
Rusch, L. C., et al. (2009b). Lines of evidence in support of FAP. In
M. Tsai, R. J. Kohlenberg, J. W. Kanter, B. Kohlenberg, W. C. Follette,
& G. M. Callaghan (eds.), *A guide to functional analytic psychotherapy:
Awareness, courage, love and behaviorism* (pp. 21–36). New York:
Springer.

Beck, A. T., Rush, A. J., Shaw, B. F., & Emery, G. (1979). *The cognitive
therapy of depression*. New York: Guilford Press.

Behavior Analysis Association of Michigan (retrieved March 15, 2011). *Behaviorism deathwatch: A collection of premature obituaries and other naive comments on the status of behaviorism*. Retrieved from http://www.baam.emich.edu/baammiscpages/baamdeathwatch.htm

Bolling, M. Y., Terry, C. M., & Kohlenberg, R. J. (2006). Behavioral theories. In J. C. Thomas, D. L. Segal, (vol. eds.), M. Herson, J. C. Thomas (eds. in chief), *Comprehensive handbook of personality and psychopathology*, volume 1: *Personality and everyday functioning* (pp. 142–157). Hoboken, NJ: John Wiley.

Boring, E. G., Bridgman, P. W., Feige, H., Pratt, C. C., & Skinner, B. F. (1945). Rejoinders and second thoughts. *Psychological Review, 52*(5), 278–294. doi: 10.1037/h0063275

Bowlby, J. (1969). *Attachment and loss*. New York: Basic Books.

Brown, B. (2010). *The power of vulnerability*. Retrieved March 15, 2011, from http://www.ted.com/talks/brene_brown_on_vulnerability.html

Brown, B. (n.d.). Retrieved March 15, 2011, from http://www.ordinarycourage.com/

Buber, M. (n.d.). *Martin Buber quotes*. Retrieved February 14, 2008, from thinkexist.com/quotes/martin_buber/

Burman, B., & Margolin, G. (1992). Analysis of the association between marital relationships and health problems: An interactional perspective. *Psychological Bulletin, 112*(1), 39–63.

Busch, A. M., Callaghan, G. C., Kanter, J. W., Baruch, D. E., & Weeks, C. E. (2010a). The Functional Analytic Psychotherapy Rating Scale: A replication and extension. *Journal of Contemporary Psychotherapy, 40*, 11–19.

Busch, A. M., Kanter, J. W., Callaghan, G. M., Baruch, D. E., Weeks, C. E., & Berlin, K. S. (2009). A micro-process analysis of functional analytic psychotherapy's mechanism of change. *Behavior Therapy, 40*, 280–290.

Busch, A. M., Manos, R. C., Rusch, L. C., Bowe, W. M., & Kanter, J. W. (2010b). FAP and behavioral activation. In J. W. Kanter, M. Tsai, & R. J. Kohlenberg (eds.), *The practice of functional analytic psychotherapy* (pp. 65–81). New York: Springer.

Callaghan, G. M. (2006a). The Functional Idiographic Assessment Template (FIAT) system: For use with interpersonally-based interventions including Functional Analytic Psychotherapy (FAP) and FAP-enhanced treatments. *The Behavior Analyst Today, 7*, 357–398.

Callaghan, G. M. (2006b). Functional analytic psychotherapy and supervision. *International Journal of Behavioral and Consultation Therapy, 2*, 416–431.

Callaghan, G. M., Gregg, J. A., Marx, B., Kohlenberg, B. S., & Gifford, E. (2004). FACT: The utility of an integration of Functional Analytic Psychotherapy and Acceptance and Commitment Therapy to alleviate human suffering. *Psychotherapy: Theory, Research, Practice, Training*, *41*, 195–207.

Clark, D. A., Beck, A. T., & Alford, B. A. (1999). *Scientific foundations of cognitive theory and therapy of depression*. New York: John Wiley.

Cordova, J. V., & Scott, R. L. (2001). Intimacy: A behavioral interpretation. *Behavior Analyst*, *24*(1), 75–86.

Deikman, A. J. (1973). The meaning of everything. In R. E. Ornstein (ed.), *The nature of human consciousness* (pp. 317–326). San Francisco, CA: Freeman.

Dichter, G., Felder, J., Petty, C., Bizzell, J., Ernst, M., & Smoski, M. J. (2009). The effects of psychotherapy on neural responses to rewards in major depression. *Biological Psychiatry*, *66*(9), 886–897.

Edwards, C. E., & Murdock, N. L. (1994). Characteristics of therapist self-disclosure in the counseling process. *Journal of Counseling and Development*, *72*, 384–389.

Erikson, E. (1968). *Identity, youth, and crisis*. New York: Norton.

Ethical Principles of Psychologists and Code of Conduct, 2010 Amendments (2010). Retrieved January 2, 2011, from http://www.apa.org/ethics/code/index.aspx

Feminist Code of Ethics (1999). Retrieved April 15, 2011, from http://www.chrysaliscounseling.org/Feminist_Therapy.html

Ferster, C. B. (1967). The transition from laboratory to clinic. *The Psychological Record*, *17*, 145–150.

Follette, W. C., & Callaghan, G. M. (1995). Do as I do, not as I say: A behavior-analytic approach to supervision. *Professional Psychology: Research & Practice*, *26*, 413–421.

Follette, W. C., Naugle, A. E., & Callaghan, G. M. (1996). A radical behavioral understanding of the therapeutic relationship in effecting change. *Behavior Therapy*, *27*(4), 623–641.

Gable, S. L. & Reis, H.T. (2006). Intimacy and the self: An iterative model of the self and close relationships. In P. Noller & J. Feeney (eds.), *Close relationships: Functions, forms and processes* (pp. 211–225). London: Psychology Press.

Green Politics (n.d.). Retrieved March 15, 2008, from http://en.wikipedia.org/wiki/Green_movement

Gurman, A. S., Waltz, T. J., & Follette, W. C. (2010). FAP-enhanced couple therapy: Perspectives and possibilities. In J. W. Kanter, M. Tsai & R. J. Kohlenberg (eds.), *The practice of functional analytic psychotherapy* (pp. 125–147). New York: Springer.

Haggbloom, S. J., Warnick, R., Warnick, J. E., Jones, V. K., Yarbrough, G. L., Russell, T. M., et al. (2002). The 100 most eminent psychologists of the 20th century. *Review of General Psychology, 6*, 139–152.

Hayes, S. C. (1984). Making sense of spirituality. *Behaviorism, 12*(2), 99–110.

Hayes, S. C., Barnes-Holmes, D., & Roche, B. (eds.) (2001). *Relational frame theory: A post-Skinnerian account of human language and cognition.* New York: Kluwer Academic/Plenum Publishers.

Hayes, S. C., & Brownstein, A. J. (1986). Mentalism, behavior–behavior relations, and a behavior-analytic view of the purposes of science. *Behavior Analyst, 9*(2), 175–190.

Hayes, S. C., & Hayes, L. J. (1992). Some clinical implications of contextualistic behaviorism: The example of cognition. *Behavior Therapy, 23*(2), 225–249.

Hayes, S. C., Hayes, L. J., & Reese, H. W. (1988). Finding the philosophical core: A review of Stephen C. Pepper's world hypotheses: A study in evidence. *Journal of the Experimental Analysis of Behavior, 50*(1), 97–111.

Hayes, S. C., Strosahl, K. D., & Wilson, K. G. (1999). *Acceptance and commitment therapy: An experiential approach to behavior change.* New York: Guilford Press.

Hill, C. E., Helms, J. E., Tichenor, V., Spiegel, S. B., O'Grady, K. E., & Perry, E. S. (1988). The effects of therapist response modes in brief psychotherapy. *Journal of Counseling Psychology, 35*, 222–233.

Hoekstra, R., & Tsai, M. (2010). FAP for interpersonal process groups. In J. W. Kanter, M. Tsai, & R. J. Kohlenberg (eds.), *The practice of functional analytic psychotherapy* (pp. 247–260). New York: Springer.

Horvath, A. O. (2001). The alliance. *Psychotherapy, 38*(4), 365–372.

Houston, M. A., Apsche, J. A., & Bass, C. K. (2007). A comprehensive literature review of Mode Deactivation Therapy. *International Journal of Behavioral Consultation and Therapy, 3*(2), 271–309.

Kanter, J. W. (2010, October). *Functional Analytic Psychotherapy (FAP): A micro-process approach to evaluating the mechanism of change of psychotherapy.* Invited lecture for the 2010 Australia–New Zealand ACBS (ACT & RFT) Conference, Adelaide, Australia.

Kanter, J. W., Kohlenberg, R. J., & Loftus, E. F. (2004). Experimental and psychotherapeutic demand characteristics and the cognitive therapy rationale: An analogue study. *Cognitive Therapy and Research, 28*(2), 229–239.

Kanter, J. W., Landes, S. J., Busch, A. M., Rusch, L. C., Brown, K. R., Baruch, D. E., et al. (2006). The effect of contingent reinforcement on target variables in outpatient psychotherapy for depression: A successful and unsuccessful case using functional analytic psychotherapy. *Journal of Applied Behavior Analysis, 39*, 463–467.

Kanter, J. W., Weeks, C. E., Bonow, J. T., Landes, S. J., Callaghan, G. M., & Follette, W. C. (2009). Assessment and case conceptualization. In M. Tsai, R. J. Kohlenberg, J. W. Kanter, B. Kohlenberg, W. C. Follette, & G. M. Callaghan (eds.), *A guide to functional analytic psychotherapy: awareness, courage, love and behaviorism* (pp. 37–59). New York: Springer.

Kazantzis, N., & Lampropoulos, G. K. (2002). Reflecting on homework in psychotherapy: What can we conclude from research and experience? *Journal of Clinical Psychology, 58*, 577–585.

Knox, S., & Hill, C. E. (2003). Therapist self-disclosure: Research based suggestions for practitioners. *Journal of Clinical Psychology/In Session, 59*, 529–539.

Kohlenberg, B. S., & Callaghan, G. M. (2010). FAP and acceptance commitment therapy (ACT): Similarities, divergence, and integration. In J. W. Kanter, M. Tsai, & R. J. Kohlenberg (eds.), *The practice of functional analytic psychotherapy* (pp. 31–46). New York: Springer.

Kohlenberg, R. J., Kanter, J. W., Bolling, M. Y., Parker, C., & Tsai, M. (2002). Enhancing cognitive therapy for depression with functional analytic psychotherapy: Treatment guidelines and empirical findings. *Cognitive and Behavioral Practice, 9*(3), 213–229.

Kohlenberg, R. J., Kanter, J. W., Tsai, M., & Weeks, C. E. (2010). FAP and cognitive behavior therapy. In J. W. Kanter, M. Tsai, & R. J. Kohlenberg (eds.), *The practice of functional analytic psychotherapy* (pp. 11–30). New York: Springer.

Kohlenberg, R. J., Kohlenberg, B., & Tsai, M. (2009a). Intimacy. In M. Tsai, R. J. Kohlenberg, J. W. Kanter, B. Kohlenberg, W. C. Follette, & G. M. Callaghan (eds.), *A guide to functional analytic psychotherapy: Awareness, courage, love and behaviorism* (pp. 131–144), New York: Springer.

Kohlenberg, R. J., & Tsai, M. (1991). *Functional analytic psychotherapy: Creating intense and curative therapeutic relationships*. New York: Plenum Press.

Kohlenberg, R. J., & Tsai, M. (1994). Functional analytic psychotherapy: A radical behavioral approach to treatment and integration. *Journal of Psychotherapy Integration, 4*(3), 175–201.

Kohlenberg, R. J., Tsai, M., Kanter, J. W., & Parker, C. R. (2009b). Self and mindfulness. In M. Tsai, R. J. Kohlenberg, J. W. Kanter, B. Kohlenberg, W. C. Follette, & G. M. Callaghan (eds.), *A guide to functional analytic psychotherapy: Awareness, courage, love and behaviorism* (pp. 103–130). New York: Springer.

Kohut, H. (1971). *The analysis of the self.* New York: International Universities Press.

Lejuez, C. W., Hopko, D. R., Acierno, R., Daughters, S. B., & Pagoto, S. L. (2011). Ten year revision of the brief behavioral activation treatment for depression: Revised treatment manual. *Behavior Modification, 35*(2), 111–161.

Linehan, M. M. (1993). *Cognitive-behavioral treatment of borderline personality disorder.* New York: Guilford Press.

Longmore, R. J., & Worrell, M. (2007). Do we need to challenge thoughts in cognitive behavior therapy? *Clinical Psychology Review, 27*(2), 173–187.

Luciano, M. (1999). Acceptance and commitment therapy (ACT) and functional analytic psychotherapy (FAP): Foundations, characteristics, and precautions. *Analisis y Modificacion de Conducta, 25*(102), 497–584.

Manos, R. C., Kanter, J. W., Rusch, L. C., Turner, L. B., Roberts, N. A., & Busch, A. M. (*2009*). Integrating Functional Analytic Psychotherapy and Behavioral Activation for the treatment of relationship distress. *Clinical Case Studies, 8*, 122–138.

Mansfield, A. K., & Cordova, J. V. (2007). A behavioral perspective on adult attachment style, intimacy and relationship health. In D. Woods & J. Kanter (eds.), *Understanding behavior disorders: A contemporary behavioral perspective* (pp. 389–416). Reno: Context Press.

Martell, C. R., Dimidjian, S., & Herman-Dunn, R. (2010). *Behavioral activation for depression: A clinician's guide.* New York: Guilford.

Masterson, J. F. (1985). *The real self.* New York: Brunner/Mazel.

Mehta, S., & Farina, A. (1997). Is being "sick" really better? Effect of the disease view of mental disorders on stigma. *Journal of Social and Clinical Psychology, 16*, 405–419.

Meyer, B., & Pilkonis, P.A. (2001). Attachment style. *Psychotherapy, 38*(4), 466–472.

Milne, D., & James, I. (2000). A systematic review of effective cognitive-behavioral therapies: Similarities and differences. *Journal of Cognitive Psychotherapy, 12*, 95–108.

Nichols, M. P., & Efran, J. (1985). Catharsis in psychotherapy: a new perspective. *Psychotherapy: Theory, Research and Practice, 22*(1), 46–58.

Pielage, S. B., Luteijn, F., & Arrindell, W. A. (2005). Adult attachment, intimacy and psychological distress in a clinical and community sample. *Clinical Psychology & Psychotherapy, 12*(6), 455–464.

Read, J., & Harre, N. (2001). The role of biological and genetic causal beliefs in the stigmatization of "mental patients". *Journal of Mental Health, 10,* 223–236.

Rogers, C. R. (1961). *On becoming a person.* Boston: Houghton Mifflin.

Rosenfarb, I. S. (2010). FAP and psychodynamic therapies. In J. W. Kanter, M. Tsai, & R. J. Kohlenberg (eds.), *The practice of functional analytic psychotherapy* (pp. 83–95). New York: Springer.

Russell, R., & Wells, P. A. (1994). Predictors of happiness in married couples. *Personality and Individual Differences, 17*(3), 313–321.

Safran, J. D., & Muran, J. C. (2001). A relational approach to training and supervision in cognitive psychotherapy. *Journal of Cognitive Psychotherapy, 15,* 3–15.

Shapiro, J. L. (1987). Message from the masters on breaking old ground? The Evolution of Psychotherapy Conference. *Psychotherapy in Private Practice, 5*(3), 65–72.

Sharpley, C. F. (2010). A review of the neurobiological effects of psychotherapy for depression. *Psychotherapy: Theory, Research, Practice, Training, 47*(4), 603–615.

Skinner, B. F. (1953). *Science and human behavior.* New York: Macmillan.

Skinner, B. F. (1957). *Verbal behavior.* East Norwalk, CT: Appleton-Century-Crofts.

Skinner, B. F. (1974). *About behaviorism.* New York: Knopf.

Skinner, B. F. (1976). *Walden two.* New Jersey: Prentice Hall. (Original work published 1948.)

Truax, C. B. (1966). Reinforcement and nonreinforcement in Rogerian psychotherapy. *Journal of Abnormal Psychology, 71*(1), 1–9.

Tsai, M., Callaghan, G. M., Kohlenberg, R. J., Follette, W. C., & Darrow, S. M. (2009a). Supervision and therapist self-development. In M. Tsai, R. J. Kohlenberg, J. W. Kanter, B. Kohlenberg, W. C. Follette, & G. M. Callaghan (eds.), *A guide to functional analytic psychotherapy: Awareness, courage, love and behaviorism* (pp. 167–198). New York: Springer.

Tsai, M., Kohlenberg, R. J., Bolling, M. Y., & Terry, C. (2009b). Values in therapy and Green FAP. In M. Tsai, R. J. Kohlenberg, J. W. Kanter, B. Kohlenberg, W. C. Follette, & G. M. Callaghan (eds.), *A guide to functional analytic psychotherapy: Awareness, courage, love and behaviorism.* (pp. 199–212). New York: Springer.

Tsai, M., Kohlenberg, R. J., Kanter, J. W., Kohlenberg, B., Follette, W. C., & Callaghan, G. M. (2009c). *A guide to functional analytic psychotherapy: Awareness, courage, love and behaviorism.* New York: Springer.

Tsai, M., Kohlenberg, R. J., Kanter, J. W., & Waltz, J. (2009d). Therapeutic techniques: The five rules. In M. Tsai, R. J. Kohlenberg, J. W. Kanter, B. Kohlenberg, W. C. Follette, & G. M. Callaghan (eds.), *A guide to functional analytic psychotherapy: Awareness, courage, love and behaviorism* (pp. 61–102). New York: Springer.

Tsai, M., Plummer, M., Kanter, J., Newring, R., & Kohlenberg, R. (2010). Therapist grief and Functional Analytic Psychotherapy: Strategic self-disclosure of personal loss. *Journal of Contemporary Psychotherapy*, *40*(1), 1–10.

Vandenberghe, L., Tsai, M., Valero, L., Ferro, R., Kerbauy, R., Wielenska, R., et al. (2010). Transcultural FAP. In J. W. Kanter, M. Tsai & R. J. Kohlenberg (eds.), *The practice of functional analytic psychotherapy.* (pp. 173–185). New York: Springer.

Van Orden, K., Wingate, L. R., Gordon, K. H., & Joiner, T. E. (2005). Interpersonal factors as vulnerability to psychopathology over the life course. In B. L. Hankin & J. R. Z. Abela (eds.), *Development of psychopathology: A vulnerability-stress perspective* (pp. 136–160). Thousand Oaks, CA: Sage Publications.

Waltz, J., Landes, S. J., & Holman, G. I. (2010). FAP and dialectical behavior therapy (DBT). In J. W. Kanter, M. Tsai, & R. J. Kohlenberg (eds.), *The practice of functional analytic psychotherapy* (pp. 47–64). New York: Springer.

Watkins, C. E., Jr (1990). The effects of counselor self-disclosure: A research review. *The Counseling Psychologist*, *18*, 477–500.

Watson, J. B. (1930). *Behaviorism* (revised edition). Chicago, IL: University of Chicago Press.

Index